Contents

Volume 97:1 Spring 2007

Poems

Centrefold

Reviews & Prizes

Endpapers

POEMS

Novelty, gorgeousness, lament.
—Moniza Alvi

David Harsent
Necrophilia

No wayward promise, nothing to shake the heart,
nothing to warm to, no trace of harm or hurt,

nothing of jealousy, no risk of bliss,
the wide, white eye; the perfect parting kiss.

Sean O'Brien
Blue Night

Blue night. Enormous Arctic air. Orion's belt.
A geostationary satellite.
The birds all sheltering or flown.

The world is North, and turns its North Face
Pitilessly everywhere,
As deep as Neptune, local as the moon.

First came the fall and then the metaphor.
No other island, then. No gift of grace.
For this alone is 'seriously there'.

Therefore. Therefore. Do not be weak.
They have no time for pity or belief,
The heavens, in their triumph of technique.

The Them

They like to do the leaving. You're what's left.
Forever on the phone for Lebensraum,
They're outraged: is this world so understaffed
It cannot meet the needs of the elect?
Where are the engineered consent, the odalisques,
To match these selfless gifts of steaming Zaum?
And these insane requests to be ignored:
What did you seriously expect?
Look now: the tanks are massing on your desk;
The gods must be garrotted or adored.

Medbh McGuckian
Mariola With Angel Choir

In the shrill turquoise air
Of first century Palestine
The rough-hewn cross is already
Regenerating: lily crucifix.

Jesus's lips are a winestock:
His Z-bend, the ropelike winding
Of his legs, are provocations
To the senses. He is smiling

Almost as broadly as the pet
Swan on his foot rest – his keynote
Above all is assurance –
Bells and fragrances.

What strikes now is the sudden
Glory of his smile in its measured
Beauty, and the smiling
Of his censing angels, an array

Of thirty bust-length
Jubilant and psalmodic,
Great and trumpeting,
Colossal and tremendous angels:

Angel with Crown of Thorns,
(Meaning whether herbs or harmonies
Are capable of preventing
A demon from afflicting mankind),

Angel with Hawk, Lure and Gauntlets,
Angel with Bird of Prey, playing
A game with a hood, the frowning
Angel of the Expulsion.

Some slim and lithe, others
Squat, one so fat as to seem
Incapable of flight – one mighty angel,
The Angel of the Millstone.

Weighty, ample figures,
Prodigious and surprising,
In their magnificent ranks
And zestful deviations.

In their hilaritas, their buoyant
Musicality, their multiplicity,
Their dazzling, swift and powerful
Intelligences sharpening language

With their final vocabularies:
Strong, resident angels,
Vigilant, secreted angels,
Imported to stand on colonnettes

And crown the sacred kings of England;
Greeting the precocious dawn
Near the East window with its Northern
French geometry whereby one might

Be seduced by it, and seduction
Become rapture. (In summer especially,
The progressive illumination
During the dawn office of Lauds.)

The ninth order of angels, assuming
In their bustling jollity the wings
Of the morning: still alert to this church
And its clumsy prayer, rotated

To their nimble and peculiar
Fingertips, spectacular and outspread,
Facing away in their strange idiom,
The spinning of the angels called virtues.

Dyad, No.3

I have the feeling of being touched out
By hands as hard as wood, my insufficient
Milk overwhelmingly white in this peeling
Gold-vanilla centrefold. Slow and fast colours
Of the black city leave embossed prints
Of shadows cast by world-wide October light,
Where two hills next the sea form a heart
Of comely streets wharfed with worldly industry.

I think how infants sleep across the globe; the bio-
Underclass, how they wear their babies to improve
The latch, of watery foremilk and creamy hindmilk
Before the true milk comes in. The dust
That undergirds, collecting on their bodies,
Is answered by my dark-red audience, the leaves.

Ciaran Carson
A Couple Of Words

Ce n'est pas comme le pain de Paris. There's no stretch in it,
you said. It was our anniversary, whether first or last.

It's the matter of the texture. Elasticity.
The crust should crackle when you break the *baton.* Then you pull

the crumb apart to make skeins full of holes. I was grappling
with your language over the wreck of the dinner table.

The maitre d' was looking at us in a funny way
as if he caught the drift I sought between the lines you spoke.

For one word never came across as just itself, but you
would put it over as insinuating something else.

Then slowly, slowly we would draw in on one another
until everything was implicated like wool spooled

from my yawning hands as you wound the yarn into a ball.
For how many seasons have we circled round each other

Like this? Was it because you came from there and I from here?
That said, before we were a gleam in someone else's eye?

Behind the screen of reasons, how much further back we go.
La nuit s'approche, you said, and then I saw the parish church

below the Alps of those three words, and snow falling, a bell
tolling as their farewells dimmed into the gathering dusk.

Our two candles were guttering by now. We climbed the stair
and found ourselves spreadeagled on the patchwork double quilt

following the dips and gradients of the staggered repeats
four maiden aunts had stitched into it fifty years before

the Last War, one of them your ancestor. So you had been told
as you told me that day in Paris we two first ventured

under it, into the future we would make together
there and then, the bread you bought that morning not yet broken.

Hotel Del Mar

Sound of waves without. You were abroad and ignorant in
the tongue you heard whispering from a dinner table more

than one remove away from you, two pairs of lips closing
in on one another in the flickering candlelight –

murmuring of sweet nothings, you surmised, since it was Greek
to you. Waves on the beach. Did we two, you wondered, ever

come across like that? Some lonely traveller to overhear
words not understood, a shadow on the periphery?

Whatever window opened then, moonlight shivered on you,
the gold crushed velvet curtains stirred in the breeze off the sea.

The couple spoke more boldly now, as if you were not there.
So you told it that I might fathom the deep of its sound,

we two seas foundering into one another over
the neck of a peninsula, making it an island.

David Harsent
from Broken Glass (2)

A word unsaid, a withdrawal, a second guess
right at the wrong time...
The dry *clack-clack* of the abacus.

ॐ

After all that, milady's final choice:
'Not bloodstone – *moon*stone.' And then:
'They say my true instrument is voice.'

ॐ

Waking, again, in tears for the moment lost
to the moment of waking;
all day long you walk with that same ghost.

ॐ

The footfall of the uninvited guest.
The EntriCam.
Teeth and hair and pixillated lust.

ॐ

The colour green, as if no other colour would do.
She was going through snow for sure,
so a long time back. So it might have been brown or blue.

ॐ

A stipple of spit on the tiling. A snatch
of song. Machinery cranking up.
Rain-clouds as far as... Catnap. Mix and match.

ℬ

Cock-crow. Clean linen. A sea-mist.
Tulips one side of a limestone wall.
Given time, I could complete this list.

ℬ

A man steps off a tall building. Your task?
To remember the slinky undertone
of shoe-leather on brick; not much to ask.

ℬ

This word from the edge of sleep: *abandonment.*
Oh, very clear since you ask.
And clearer still what it meant.

ℬ

She could touch you now, if she wanted. She could find
the little rub of blue where she touched you last,
not a bruise, exactly; not quite. She could do it blind.

Tomas Venclova
Lake District

The moment you open the door, everything falls into place –
the little steamer by the wharf, the firs and the thujas.
The old hag feeding the ducks might in fact be as old as Leni
Riefenstahl. At the foot of the hill, the chestnuts in early bloom
are a bit younger, probably of the same age as her films.
All is wet and bright. A hedgehog or only God knows whose
soul is rummaging through yesteryear's leaves. The dead water and the
                                                               water

of life fill the plain; both Celsius and Fahrenheit
predict a fine spring day; a shadow covers up
the past (and the present too); the first serene weeks
burnish the bridges, as it were, with emery
in a peaceful corner of Europe between Wannsee and Potsdam –
where so much has happened, and where nothing more, it seems, will
                                                               happen.
For days on end we've been seeing a mangy crow – in the garden,
sometimes on the roof. The ancients would have said
that her determination is a prophecy. Having emerged out of the thick
of the trees, it skips from one antenna crossbar
to another, its sides glistening like quicksilver
in a thermometer's tube. We are unable to understand
what these scale marks mean. Perhaps the onset of agony?
The past does not enlighten, but it still attempts
to say something. It may be that the crow knows more about us
and about the filth of history than we do ourselves.
What does it want to remind us of? Black photographs, black headphones
of radio operators, black signatures on documents,
the frozen stare of the unarmed, the prisoner's boot or the trunk
of the refugee? Probably not. This we remember anyway,
and it won't add to our wisdom. The bird is only symbol
of patience and perseverance. Ask for them,
and your petition will be granted.

Dunes At Watermill

Some six or seven time zones (I'm not sure
about the exact number) separate
us from the continent, which has by now
turned into postal codes and silence. Say,
Long Island: water-polished pebbles, a rough-
hewn wooden pier – the long-familiar view –
a sleepless clear horizon, boats and sails.
The lagoon's elbows touch the barn, the grass.
From here you cannot see the ocean, but
you know it's there: the glimmer of the surf
is barely audible, waves flinging foam
and flakes of jellyfish at footprints (our own
perhaps). The lengthening day wedges into
the door of the garage and leaves a more
permanent mark: the undulating longhand
of tyres which gleams with moisture like a fresh
fingerprint on an application form.
A discontented airplane taints the azure.
Only seagulls are motionless. Commercials
harass the screen, but it has seen far worse.
A shade descends the stairs. Our host attends to
the stove like a witch doctor, dumping out
oysters and shrimp into the boiling water,
his fingers shaky, more than they were last year,
that being the only piece of news on this
island of lotus-eaters. After four
we'll all go to the local bookstore where
his twelve friends will pay tribute to his poems
with humble applause. I never asked him where
he had been born. He's not a stranger to
the province I come from (that much I know),
and neither are his listeners, hailing from
adjacent time zones and a common landscape.

Different destinies. Take V., who's sitting
in the far corner, blinded by the sun.
He still remembers how, years since, he tripped
over the bumps and potholes of the road
as he was running to the terminal.
Like a mirage, it kept receding further
away and further between walls of concrete.
The consul was no longer on the platform.
He had been fired two days (or hours) before.
But he *was* there, in the compartment, busy.
He leaned out of the coach's window just
in time to put his clumsy signature
on the life-saving papers and was off.
A different lot fell to A.S., the son
of an attorney (a professor now).
They seized him near the border (a scar marks
the bayonet wound on his shoulder). Later
he rooted bushes out and chopped down trees
in the taiga, becoming an accomplished
lumberjack who did work for two: his mother
didn't have the strength to do men's work. At last,
they fled to freedom through Iran, but that's
another story. The psychiatrist M.
doesn't like to talk about the stinky hole
where he (one of the twenty-seven men
out of five hundred) got away from death.
The guards disbanded and the barbed wire snapped
when a tank rolled into the prison camp.
The strident liberator turned into
a warden before long, but in those days,
thank God, they could still slip away from him,
even those who'd died on more than one occasion.

My friend is driving us back home, his heavy
hand resting on the steering wheel. (Not much
has changed since last year.) He knows more, perhaps,
than all of us. I also come from there.
I didn't fell trees and didn't faint in the barracks,
but I was born there too, in the same time zone.
If continents change, they do so much too slowly.
Our retinas must contain identical
imprints, although it may be that where they
had seen a brick wall or a street lamp, I
saw emptiness. I've lived through the last third
part of this century, and yet I've seen
enough of it. But here's the house. We're back.
In front of us, the ivy-covered poles,
the wooden wall smeared with fresh paint all over,
and, on the cool lawn, a newspaper with
fresh pictures from the Balkan front.

Most likely, nothing else exists besides
these fleeting traces, fragments, imprints on
the sand, the asphalt, on our consciousness,
our passports, and our bodies. The new times
advance like a relentless avalanche
and blot them out. We face old age
and death, which comes at the appointed hour,
like postcards, bills, or an unbidden guest
who interrupts a dinner of shrimp and oysters.

An empty bottle on the table. Night
sweeps up the crumbs and consummates the feast.
The town is nodding off. The motorboats'
lights and the stars commingle in the sky.
A ray of light touches the shelf, and swans
take off for Canada in V-formations.

Translated by Constantine Rusanov

Moniza Alvi
The Veil

We thought we knew the sky
spread out above us.
But now it too is veiled.

We read newspapers through a haze.
The rose wears a veil though
it cannot shield us from its thorns.

What is the veil but a kind of partition,
light as gossamer,
or dark as the River Styx?

Behind it eggs are cracked open
and the yolks run everywhere.
All we'd ever wanted to see

flickers across its window –
a boulevard, a skating rink.
Novelty, gorgeousness, lament.

The veil with its hidden waist and hips,
its energies, its limitations.
The capacious veiled veil.

The world itself is veiled,
the receding east, the receding west.

Upholding The 'I'

I try to uphold the 'I'
to push it upright

the clear, straight 'I'
stalking onwards

or resting on its back
the horizontal 'I'
like a log across a stream

the 'I' leaning to one side,
aslant in the afternoon sun,

the best time for photographs.

*

The naked 'I' in an unused room
tall enough to peer out of the window.

The 'I' shouts for clothes
for a cloak to trail on the lakeside turf
for padded shoulders.

The 'I' has strange proportions.

*

'We' are its cousins,
its close confederates.

The 'I' crashes around,
trying to find its own way.

But what could be called 'its own' –
the arrows it shoots in the dark?

*

The 'I' is gold dust –
a crocus in the mouth

a smear of mustard
the bellow of the sun.

*

The 'I'.

No point hammering it
like a stake into the ground

or planting it in a dream
or digging it up –

*

the crooked 'I'

the 'I' that's beelike, drawn to purple

the 'I' with its walk-on part

its cool green stem

Sarah Wardle
Healing

In art therapy I do not draw a picture,
but write my name with my left hand,
Greek letters backwards, as in a mirror,
and in English, 'I can! I can! I can! I can!'

John F. Deane
Bunnacurry

There is, always, a riverbank, a flowing, stuff
of dream-beginnings, where you fished
with hacked-off stick and twine, filched hook
and torn worm, lifting an eel that poured

like a thread of molten butter onto grass,
and you dreaded it, dreaded the squirm and coil,
how it would slime around your fingers,
so that you left it, stick and twine and catch,

riverbank and muddle-pool, and ran, leaving
a river that had become scarcely a stream
when you returned, a stream so choked with fern,
thistle, bramble-reach that you can barely see

a mud-dark trickle over mud-brown stones. Everything
altered, and everything the same, familiarity
offering some consolation till you grow aware
how far you've run, how little time is left. You have learned

to name things: teasel, stonechat, quartz, have brought
someone home you cleave to, reciting
the silly stories, telling the histories of byre
hill and hedgerow till you fall silent, awed

at the smallness of this living, weighted too
with its mysteries, knowing that, after all,
your words have been this small stream's words,
your flowing this small stream's flow.

Jean Sprackland
The Birkdale Nightingale

Bufo calamito – the Natterjack toad

On Spring nights you can hear them
two miles away, calling their mates
to the breeding place, a wet slack in the dunes.
Lovers hiding nearby are surprised
by desperate music. One man searched all night
for a crashed spaceship.

For amphibians, they are terrible swimmers:
where it's tricky to get ashore, they drown.
By day they sleep in crevices under the boardwalk,
run like lizards from cover to cover
without the sense to leap when a gull snaps.
Yes, he can make himself fearsome,
inflating his lungs to double his size.
But cars on the coast road are not deterred.

She will lay a necklace of pearls in the reeds.
Next morning, a dog will run into the water and scatter them.
Or she'll spawn in a footprint filled with salt rain
that will dry to a crust in two days.

Still, when he calls her and climbs her
they are well designed. The nuptial pads on his thighs
velcro him to her back. She steadies beneath him.

The puddle brims with moonlight.
Everything leads to this.

Peter Porter
Shakespeare's Defeat

No-one has ever been his equal
Yet quizzing him in doggerel
Is any Tribune's timid right:
All language is dispersed in light.

The Ordinary sunk in ordinariness
Say he is bald and hard to guess.
The Archons think to find a focus
Might tear its petals from the crocus.

Country Wisdom's top Townee,
His coat-of-arms Complicity –
The bubo of the world when squeezed
Is odium, yet some are pleased.

The Adam Smithy of our need
Commands both vile and pedigree'd.
So Mouldy, Feeble and Bullcalf
Get pricked; the audience gets to laugh.

His works are like Miss Eman's tent –
She sleeps with all, not just the bent,
But stencilled on the flapping walls
Legitimation calls and calls.

Music does it better, so
He has a journey shortly to go
But never come to that fine palace
Up a beanstalk from the phallus.

We writers want him as our Prince
A crazy public to convince
But would he even place a bet
On redemption via the Internet?

The dark house and detested wife:
After marriage, get a life!
Start out defeated – the glory is
Your Art shall seem vitorious.

What's Playing In Eternity?

It must be separate from its maker,
his leg-gummata and the sound
of dream's Beethoven – pure
bullying of all who love
his 'none-so-great-as-me' outreach,
while the root position stays
in soul's retreat from syphilis's
demi-moral storm. The music,
like Vespasian's coins, will never smell
of anything behind the foreskin. Time
has told its fractions – use your voice,
this breaking world is crutch enough
to be a scaffold for the nowhere near.

And her inscription of despair
affords a little time to listen:
she was devoted to a more
oblivious obsession, yet some days
there would be space for music
and a favourite piece would play
among the circling furniture,
beyond the deafness of drawn curtains.
Strange that I can see them, stepping from
the record sleeve, three nuns in habits,
inhabiting E Flat,
empowered as angels to command
a truth more generous than love's.

Gwyneth Lewis
from How To Knit A Poem

How To Knit A Poem

The whole thing starts with a single knot
and needles. A word and pen. Tie a loop
in nothing. Look at it. Cast on, repeat

the procedure till you have a line
that you can work with.
It's a pattern made of relation alone,

my patience, my rhythm, till empty bights
create a fabric that can be worn,
if you're lucky and practised. It's never too late

to pick up dropped stitches, each hole a clue
to something that might be bothering you,
though I link mine with ribbons and pretend

I meant them to happen. I make a net
of meaning that I carry round
portable, to work on sound

in trains and terrible waiting rooms.
It's thought in action. It redeems
odd corners of disposable time,

making them fashion. It's the kind of work
that keeps you together. The neck's too tight,
but tell me honestly: How do I look?

Philosophy

"Knitting's like everything," it's tempting to say.
No. Knitting's like knitting. Sure, there's cosmology

in Norwegian sweaters with vertical stars,
but as science that doesn't get us far.

If space is made of superstrings
then God's a knitter and everything

is craft. Perhaps we can darn
tears in the space-time continuum

and travel down wormholes to begin
to purl in another dimension's skein.

But no. There are things you can't knit:
a spaceship. A husband, though the wish

might be strong and the softest thread
would be perfect for the hair on his head,

another, tougher, that washes well
for his pecs and abdominals. You can stitch a soul

daily and unpick mistakes,
perform some moral nip and tucks –

forgiveness. Look out. Your Frankenstein
might turn and start knitting you again.

Hypnosis Knitting

A day of wordless misery,
thorns in the heart
that refuse to budge.

No matter, I'm keeping company
with myself, though hurting,
redeeming time that was torturing me.

My grandmother's craftwork,
I suddenly see,
was self-medication,

her fanciest knitwear
anti-depressant hosiery:
a stance against her melancholy.

This pattern wants only rhythm from me:
no judging, no knowing,
just moving on

into a future. I'm working three
axes. First a new personality
made from my patience.

Second, a scarf
composed in calm,
a respite from my usual self-harm.

The third is my finest.
Look! I've unpicked
myself from my worry, a delicate stitch

into the present. No one can see
this last. Mindfulness charges the air,
arrays me in intricate gossamer.

Memorial Sweater

I'm starting my magnum opus: it will be
my memorial sweater.
I can't see yet how it will end
but it starts with ribbing made of rain
on circular needles, so that the sleeves,
when they wear out, can be replaced
like choruses: Raglan cheers or batwing sighs,
depending on circumstance. I do know
I'll have shoes for pockets, the soles worn out
from dancing, I hope, to inherited tunes
and some new. I'll have a Hall of Fame:
a panel in Aran with cameos
of Milton, Herbert. I'd like a boat
in the story – if you can knit,
splicing comes easy – and a sea
of triple waves for voyages.
I'll have a computer linked to the eyes
of Hawaiian telescopes, so I can view
the mottle of early nebulae
which will be a large feature of my work.
I'd like it to be a pleasure to wear,
not tight round the neck or under the arms.
I want Moorish whispering galleries
and orange groves, the breath of moss,
the occasional desert... I must start soon.
It's cooling and, as evening comes on
terrified, I hear soft whirrs:
the pollen-heavy moths of time.

Commissioned by BBC Radio 4. Producer: Penny Arnold

Amir Or
Plates *from* The Museum Of Time

Plate 10: Bloom

When the dead are planning their next birth
cemeteries smell like spring.

They're coming closer than dreams,
roaming away from their worlds
                                        to die into the world.

You grasp them suddenly   your body winces
when they move on past you as if you were a ghost.

The dome of the view   a blue sky, a few light clouds,
is a thin curtain   powerless to shield you.

Sounds of bells and sea-shells come close to your ears.
Every breath you take   is presence.

In spring everything reveals itself in flesh again.
Glittering mirrors hang in the wind   eyes blooming everywhere.

Plate 4: Love Bed

In the corner of the room – pleasure.   A pink tongue lapping
each drop of milk   from the cat's veins.

Fish swim the lower belly –
                        it's painful for them
but they know nothing about it   nothing at all.

The body's quiet now. It's all leftovers.
The spirit   blowing gently above it
is left to its reflection:

a mirror-bird   spreading, with difficulty,
                        a single wing.

Seán Ó Ríordáin
Catology

The cat loves her own body.
She adores stretching her limbs.
When she stretched herself tonight,
cats rained in cataracts from her.

She flows from cat to cat,
releasing them with each roll
as if she wasn't a cat, but a wheel
of cats coming and going.

She is her own catechism,
a cathedral full of herself,
stretching her whole body,
categorizing herself with pride.

I have seen scores of cats
incatinate tonight.
No, not scores, but millions
still to be catalogued out of her body.

Translated by Greg Delanty

Stephen Romer
Alas Without Constraint

Having a coke with you
        in the *Coffee Parisien*
has got to be more fun
        than trailing to an exhibition
even Picasso's *érotique*;
        and pausing with you by the café
where Pérec wrote
        tentative d'épuisment d'un lieu parisien
is more thrilling
        than littérature à contraintes;
I'd rather you took me shopping
        for a pair of two-tone shoes,
and I've never been less in the mood
        and more in need
of decorum
        and a bit of restraint
and of saying less
        and meaning more,
and of everything I preached
        but cannot practice
let alone stretched out with you
        flat on the bookshop floor
with Berryman's *Sonnets*
        'volleying blue air'
because indestructible lightheartedness
        is upon me
whose sweet rare source
        was blindingly there

Oliver Reynolds
Hodge

for Alan Vaughan Williams

The more I think of Hodge
the more he comes to mind:
the prompt-corner ledge
curlicued with peel and rind;

his barn-door smile; his gloom;
the walk-in cupboard in the pit
he dubbed his dressing-room;
the way he always spat

and polished the leather
between sole and heel,
"Watch and learn, Oliver –
no bull like army bull...";

the way he was there and not there,
watching in the wings for hours,
then ghosting on; his flop of hair
as he bowed and gave flowers.

Pascale Petit
Creation Of The Birds

after the painting by Remedios Varo

I paint birds from starlight.
The harder my art, the stronger their wings –

solar or lunar feathered, iris-barbed.
And the ultrasonic syrinx,

drawn from my violin-brush,
starts to hum when I'm lonely.

I release them while still wet, their songs
liquid and light, not meant for base ears.

Even the nests they weave in our old forests
are harmonies – temporary mouths for our trees.

Restless, they embark on great migrations,
beat against the glass of earth's cage.

Julia Butterfly Hill, Treesitter

Silence has small sounds I have learnt to listen to with my skin –
the sap's slow rise up three hundred feet of xylem. Here,

where the winds make harps of needle-plumes,
morning bathes me in musical mists. Below me, birds

stretch their wings in shivering shoals of green amber.
Beneath them, the fluted trunk plunges to an earth

I have not stepped on for two years. The first few months
of my treesit they tried scaring me out with choppers,

stopped me from sleeping with floodlights, air-horns, whistles.
But my mind grew a fireproof bark. One by one,

I have watched the great trees fall all around mine in the grove.
What I remember most is the moment the chainsaw

is switched off – that different silence, as if each
of my neighbour's leaves is holding its breath

before releasing a gasp – a trembling that spirals down
to the cut. Years reel as its rings just stand there shaking.

Arne Johnsson
Three Pieces

I see your tongue, the birdsong flows around me, I go to the laundry, thinking about snow falling. The water, even if it's hidden, makes itself known in rooms and shapes. Swans call out, bells from the railway, they hook into each other. The little songbirds' throats, feathered, with muscles, running fluids, contract and extend: they, their voices and that about which they sing, that which at the extreme tip of the tongue in the end is that which leaves the body and the will: the statement, the call

 B

your tongue hidden, the houses along the streets, lingering shapes in gardens. You run your fingers over inflorescences, petals so tender that the skin can't see their weight. Breathe towards me. No one knows the other's voice within. Here you sing, humming as if working; of wings the air is full, so lightly you against me

*

so lightly you against me, visible but also invisible: silver that shimmered the backs of fish in the stream, the mosquitoes' whining, the grasses' roughness on the marshy tufts, gooseberries, barberry, juniper, gravel – in my childhood summer was a tale of summer. Once I stood alone on the steps, it was late at night, darkness fell and the heat left the ground. The wind moved through the tops of the pines and above them the stars were lit one after the other, cluster upon cluster, the shining dots assembled into a sparkling cover. When I now think of this my heart is filled with distance, light through life and memory, yes growing in my memory like first flowers then berries and fruit envelop trees and herbs with scent, flavours that cling, joined together, to hands, arms, clothes, in the mouth like covers of that – like in the water, in the air – which I see and see not

B

dreamed about falling, dreamed I was dreaming, falling through dream
after dream. I step outside, in spite of the glare the wind is cutting. I wrap
my jacket tight about me as I stroll down towards the lake. I am dazzled,
in the light I see only the light:

one who is by the water tells his child about fishes, saying that they are
there and that if we could touch the surface like we do the skin we would
feel their movements like currents and trembles to the fingertips and the
palm of the hand:

in my profession I let signs, papers change places with other, every day
the new wash over the old. Children rush through the streets, flights of
birds drift in the wind; you, what is yours, your name – I find you and I
do not find you, I touch the things gently with my hand

Translated by Katarina Trodden, Arne Johnson and Lars Ahlström

Katherine Lucas Anderson
Sunset Clause

We're tired, if truth be told, we're not waiting anymore for something
Momentous to unfold, we've come and we've gone and, still here,
We're sitting out the drone of the lawnmower, its slip and slide,
Swathes it cuts, there's a rhythm to it, and then, as night descends,
More trills, but not thrills, there are very few surprises, ecstasies,
Just this steady drip, drip, singing growing louder and, soon enough,
The moon, round as usual, will ascend from where it has patiently
Waned, all day, just behind the treeline; will pop up like slow rising
Toast, conveyed by time and space, various laws of physics, will
Deepen, and redden and glow, a cold ember, but circular as a portal,
Flat, two-dimensional, like words on a page, but still able to say so
Much, just one cocked eyebrow enough, you know what you must do
And if your lids were not growing heavier, if fireflies did not bob
Ceaselessly, rise as high as the silhouetted branches, you would have
Already left, turned the other cheek, but why does no one speak up,
Has no one anything to announce, is this just another in a long line
Of ordinary days, requisite stars, planets, each in their allotted place.

Ruth Fainlight
Midland Contemporary

i

If you stand on the path leading out of the village,
with your back to the airport buildings, the pylons
hidden, the bright motorway signs too far
on the left to enter your field of vision
and the last row of houses too far to the right,

the vista towards that distant line of hills
sloping gently down to the muddy stream
in the shallow valley that lies before you, gives
little evidence of the present moment – seems
a perfect nineteenth century English landscape.

But the moment you shift your head from that one angle
or let yourself hear the traffic-roar: the endless
stream of cars, the HGVs, the freight-planes
lifting off and the holiday flights landing,
you know exactly when and where you are.

It is this interdigitation of rural and
global, industrial and contemporary – this
evidence of encroachment by an augmenting
population and its wants: consumption and
mobility – which fascinates and appals.

ii

Cattle in the shadow of cargo hangars
and new-built terminals. Virgin, Easyjet
and DHL. Sheep with fleeces darkened
to the tarnished silver of clouds emerging
from the power station's cooling towers.

And past the highway's wire-link barrier –
and barely noticed by that Mondeo's only
passenger – discordant acres of acid
yellow rape fields coruscate like molten
metal through an open furnace door.

Pain Figure

The head is enormous,
every feature magnified –
rabbit-eyed, puffy-lipped,
tongue inflamed, aching teeth;
and the hands like padded
gauntlets, fingers extended,
legs and feet water-logged
as if moon-booted –
Dr. Frankenstein' s vision;

limbs, appendages and organs
doubled, quadrupled in size
to indicate their sensitivity
to pleasure and pain, record
the network of nerve-paths
which carry the signals
like bristling roots that spread
from the stem of an ivy –
centipede-feet grappling a wall;

that blue and purple drawing
from an old book, a figure
with the proportions more
of an embryo, rubber doll
or acupuncture model
than a normal human –
recalling which, awake through
the small hours, I feel myself
become its living version.

Frances Leviston
Oilseed Rape

Americans call it canola oil, the upshot of this
almost incredibly yellow horizon

charging the clouds, like a buttercup
held close to the chin

tells if you like butter or not. And then it's gone
along with most of the profitable land

when the flyover's fled, and what remains
is the blot of a stared-at sun on the eye,

those thousands and thousands of blonde girls
bowing their heads.

Moon

Startled by the moon in the middle of the day,
same blue as the sky, like a crater in it,
for the first time in years I think of the flag
still flying there, of the men whose lives are fastened to it
even though the rest of us have turned away,

and I think of all the places I've been
in love, or happy, where I'll never go again
and probably couldn't find – that linden tree in Boston
I was lying under, watching summer's college kids
lope across the grass on their muscled brown legs,
when I suddenly headed for home.

There are bones inside my body I've never seen.

Carole Satyamurti
House Of Words

Only by leaning
against each other
weight, counter-weight
do they not fall flat
again and again.

Only like that
can they enclose space
make worlds
and split infinity
again and again.

It needs dexterity
sleight of mind
knowledge of the laws
of construction
to sustain again and again

the illusion of substance;
and it takes focus
to make them stand up;
willingness to begin
again, and again.

John Haynes
from You

for Afiniki Kyari

XXX

And *you*: a pointing word for who is there,
or was. It means not he or she, not it,
not I, nor I dissolving in a stare,
or made an actor's part, and limited
by that, or that last person to be greeted
who's not you at all yet still the one
you talk to as yourself, that everyman

who has accompanied you all this way
but must stop here, must raise a hand – to *you*,
is that? And who else is there? Well, maybe
those other representatives shot through
with I and am, those empathisers who
have nothing else, each one a candidate,
each one a soul, whose empathy is that,

who says, *I'll go with you, I'll go at least*
as far as makes no difference, old chap,
dear boy, now that there's nothing else to trust
except the child in you, and who is that?
a photo ghost: tuckbox and prepschool cap,
the train, the whistle that goes on and on
until they switch it off and note the time.

XV

Respect for somebody because they've been
alive so long, their breasts are used, they heal
the sick, they teach... *The people here, they seem –*
I know that customs aren't the same – but people
here. At home no child would dare to scramble
like that past an old man getting on
a bus and not a word from anyone.

It's not... and yes, what comes into the head
is Grandma's word, Miss Bosse's word as well:
not *civilized*, Victorian indeed,
like a *baturiya* telling the tale
that Jesus told about the word for soul
translated into earth, rock, birds, wind, weeds,
your father trudging through a cloud of seeds.

And here's the Green Man that your son's Year Three
have made for parents' evening, candle soul
through cutout eyes, dreadlocks that were spaghetti
once, his smock of lettuce leaves, a whole
red pepper of a heart, (*But how can people*
make statues of food!) and roots of ginger
for his naked clumps of feet. A leper's.

baturiya – Hausa: European woman. Etymology uncertain, but possibly from
'Victoria'.

Ben Wilkinson
Filter

Out from the quay, and the trawler heading away to foreign waters
wobbles as if an apple bobbing in the kitchen basin of All Hallows' Eve.

Its dragnet of dregs, settling on the sea's black-misted base
of low-lying cod, haddock, the monstrous sub of the deep Atlantic salmon,

almost seems to be catching the water's beady-eyed contents
as if to expel its forty-one million square miles of swallowing depression.

Returning, with so much fresh fish for tomorrow's hungry morning,
and the bulk of boat slow-shifts from foot to foot, tethered down to its
                                        cobblestone jetty.

And yet, through its own fathomless way of sunless ferment, next day
sees the sea ten strong or more, as if the trawler had never flounced

its many tons, shook its shivering skin above, the freezing depths
rippling across it. The way the ocean filters up its once salt-ridden waters

to the streams and brooks inland, or how the Egyptian cobra shed its skin,
intact, carefully rubbing its head, leaving behind a perfect replica of itself.

Nigel McLoughlin
Night Fire

and a frost of sweet winter air
goosepimples at the window
and my skin
                        bitter-warm
coffee in the mouth bursts
in the gullet, sings like a glow
inside
                        outside the moon
is just risen over the horizon
of a hedge, stars breakneck
above the yard-square
                                hedged
eight feet high on all sides,
the three walled dark shadows
age's claustrophobia
                            the city
glows around the bowl of the sky.
I circle the bonfire under
the cone of starlight
                            name
the familiars. Caolfionn
sees something else beyond
the rim of heat: an expanse
opening up full
                        of planes
and helicopters, dark and twinkling
and rockets I don't see.
                            He is
lifted up on the wing
of a cuckoo he invokes
at the end of each incantation.

He numbers us all on the wing,
draws us all up
                    where he stands
at my shoulder. Euan raises
one finger points into the void
shouts out
            into the vowel of the sky
and that too is open lipped, hemmed
on all sides by the red horizon
that stretches out and rolls back
as we all stand amazed
                            raising
one finger Adam-like towards
a god as yet un-named,
                            trying
to guess what it is each other sees.
Sky I say. *Moon* says Caolfionn.
Star says Teresa. *O* says Euan
O he says again, but surer.

John Sewell
Betrayal

After we fuck each other goodnight, she and I,
and fall asleep, you're there so vividly I don't know
whose limb I'm touching when I say: *I love you.*

So much so, that next morning when I gently
fuck her from behind – since she doesn't want to be
woken completely – neither, I realise, do I.

Adam Thorpe
Lifting The Harp

for A

Lugging it up two flights,
three of us on the job, my back
put out as usual, I think

of what we agreed in the concert
after the course, when fifteen
of you were playing at the same

time, while Israel was pounding
Lebanon again: how if you put
a row of harpists on the front

line of any war front (each
of their hands like a lover
desperate to reach the other

through the screen of cords
over and over and never
succeeding), the guns would stop.

We reach the top and straighten up,
letting it down like a great wing, wincing
at the considerable weight it takes

to make the music of angels.

CENTREFOLD

An activist poem should motivate investigation, not tell
readers what to think. —John Kinsella

It Must Change

Presidential Address, Modern Language Association: December 2006

MARJORIE PERLOFF

This year marks the centennial of Samuel Beckett's birth, and celebrations around the world have been a wonder to behold. From Buenos Aires to Tokyo, from Rio de Janeiro to Sofia, from South Africa (where Beckett did not permit his plays to be performed until Apartheid was ended) to New Zealand, from Florida State University Tallahassee to the University of Reading, from London's Barbican Theatre to the Pompidou Center in Paris, from Hamburg and Kassel and Zurich to Aix-en-Provence and Lille, from St. Petersburg to Madrid to Tel Aviv, and of course most notably in Dublin, 2006 has been Beckett's Year. Most of the festivals have included, not only performances of the plays, but lectures, symposia, readings, art exhibitions, and manuscript displays. *PARIS BECKETT 2006*, for example, co-sponsored by the French government and NYU's Center for French Civilization and Culture, has featured productions of Beckett's entire dramatic oeuvre, mounted in theatres large and small all over Paris, lectures by such major figures as the novelists-theorists Philippe Sollers and Hélène Cixous, the playwrights Arrabal and Israel Horovitz, and the philosopher Alain Badiou. To round things out, in 2007 the Pompidou Center will host a major exhibition of and on Beckett's work.

Some of these festivals had specific themes: at Reading, for example, the conference papers were devoted to language and intertextuality.[i] The web site for the Tokyo symposium, tells us that "In 1953, a Japanese student named Ando Shin-ya watched the world premiere of *En attendant Godot* at the Théatre de Babylone in Paris and was enchanted by this 'unprecedented' play. [...] Ando himself directed *Godot*'s Japanese premiere by the major Shingeki ('modern theatre') company Bungakuza in 1960. [...] The production triggered the avant-garde movement called the 'Underground Theatre', which developed into Shogekjo-Undou [...] the new wave of Japanese theatre." Appropriately enough, the Tokyo Symposium was called 'Borderless Beckett', committed, according to the website, to the notion that

---

i. See Daniella Caselli, 'Beckett at Reading 2006', *The Beckett Circle/Le Cercle de Beckett*, Newsletter of the Beckett Society, 29, no. 2 (Fall 2006), 2–3. I draw on accounts of some of the other festivals described in this issue.

"Beckett's art [...] undermines dualistic differences between English and French, geographical and political differences, and conventional frameworks of philosophy and aesthetics." [ii]

Who, indeed, more global an artist than Beckett? On the Los Angeles Chicano blog *La Bloga* (the recipient of *Tu Ciudad Magazine's* "Best Blog 2006" award) Michael Sedano, a regular *La Bloga* reviewer and commentator, recently posted a piece called 'Reading/Waiting for *Godot* in Translation' (21 November 2006). The occasion was two-fold: the visit to UCLA of the Dublin Gate Theatre and the publication of the new Grove Press edition of *Godot* with Beckett's French original (1952) and his English translation (1954) on facing pages. "What in the world," Sedano asks, "is a Chicano critic doing writing about Samuel Beckett?" And he explains:

> I'd never read *Godot* in French, and even if I had, I doubt I would have done a cross-cultural reading. What a perplexing bit of fun I'm having. So much, I recommend you do likewise. (Sidebar: I speak and read French as a result of the University of California's absurd rule that Spanish was not an academic language in 1963, so the language of Cervantes, my grandparents, and my parents, was forbidden for graduation credit. Chingao!") [iii]

Sedano becomes absorbed in the curious disparities between the French and English texts. "On the left, Pozzo asks Lucky, simply, if Lucky understands; in English Lucky gets called hog." "Quien sabe," says Sedano, "but sabes que, it's going to be puro fun attending the performance." And the comments from guest columnists reinforce this motif, with Manuel L. sending in a citation from *Endgame's* Clov – "I use the words you taught me / If they don't mean anything anymore, / teach me others. Or let me be silent" – and another blogger, this one anonymous, remarking, "Beckett is a Chicano! Loved your post."

As for the Dublin Gate performance itself, Design for Sharing, the programme that brings Inner City children from K through 12 to concerts, dance recitals, and theatre at UCLA, sponsored a workshop on *Godot* by Barry McGovern, which was judged to be one of the highlights of the year. The students who attended were evidently sitting on the edge of their seats, especially during the following famously absurd dialogue in Act 1:

ii. http://beckettjapan.org/borderless2.htm
iii. Michael Sedano, 'Reading/ Waiting for Godot in Translation', *La Bloga*, 21 November 2006
http://labloga.blogspot.com/2006/1

[*Silence. Estragon looks attentively at the tree.*]

VLADIMIR: What do we do now?

ESTRAGON: Wait.

VLADIMIR: Yes, but while waiting.

ESTRAGON: What about hanging ourselves?

VLADIMIR: Hmmm. It'd give us an erection.

ESTRAGON: [highly excited] An erection!

VLADIMIR: With all that follows. Where it falls mandrakes grow. That's why they shriek when you pull them up. Did you not know that?

ESTRAGON: Let's hang ourselves immediately.

VLADIMIR: From a bough? [They go toward the tree.] I wouldn't trust it.[iv]

The mandrake reference in this passage, with its allusive network to the Crucifixion, to occult legends in which mandrakes are said to utter human screams as they are pulled from the earth, and to John Donne's famous little song "Go and catch a falling star / Get with child a mandrake root," would hardly be accessible to a student audience, but the inconsequentiality of Didi's speech and Gogo's equally unexpected reaction evidently charmed the audience.

ℬ

What does all this have to do with the MLA and with our role as teachers and students of language and literature? How, for example, does the intense global literary activity I have been describing relate to the current picture of the profession as gleaned from the 2006 MLA Job Information List?[v] Suppose, for example, I am a newly minted PhD in English who wrote her thesis on some aspect of Beckett – his plays? novels? poetry? film? – or more broadly on Modern British and Irish literature and culture? Studying the lists carefully, I came up with the following numbers. There are six advertised positions in Modern British Literature, no field specified. You will agree that, given the wealth of British writing in the twentieth century, my chances are not exactly good. There are, further, three positions in Modern Drama, no nationality specified, and two each in British/Irish drama and

---

iv. Samuel Beckett, *En Attendant Godot / Waiting for Godot, A Bilingual Edition* (New York: Grove Press, 2006), 43.

v. The JIL (Job Information List), available through the MLA, is a searchable electronic database of full-time academic job openings in postsecondary departments of English and foreign languages, both in the U.S. and abroad. The database is updated weekly.

British fiction respectively. That makes thirteen positions of which one is in Singapore and three are at Canadian universities, where, as a U.S. citizen, my chances would probably be slim. Indeed, given such lean pickings, the odds of my getting any sort of tenure-track (or even non tenure-track) job in 2006 are very slight indeed.

How can there be such a disconnect between what writers and scholars at home and abroad seem to be doing and the availability of teaching positions in English literature? Who, after all, are the many students and professors who gave papers at Reading and Dublin, Lille and Aix-en-Provence, Rio and Tokyo, Tallahassee and Atlanta? The answer, my survey of speakers reveals, is that participants are established senior scholars on the one hand, graduate students on the other. What is missing is what the AAUP now calls 'replacement faculty', the new assistant professoriat that will come up through the ranks.

The dearth of entry-level jobs in language and literature is by now a familiar story, and I shall not dwell on it here, except to say that such jobs as exist are especially unlikely to go to candidates who have written their dissertations on a single author. Out in the world beyond the academy, individual poets are warmly celebrated: witness this past November's three-day Frank O'Hara Festival in New York, sponsored by Poets' House, St. Mark's Poetry Center, and the Museum of Modern Art. But dissertation topics? At Stanford, of the forty-nine dissertations completed between 2000 and 2006, exactly one deals with a single author, Henry James. But it is not just the rejection of the individual author, of 'genius theory', that has become *de rigueur*. Of the remaining forty-eight dissertations, only a handful have any specifically *literary* component, typical titles being ones like the following: 'The Garden and the Crop, Revising Rural Labor in the United States Urban Imagination, 1870-1915', 'Offending Lives: Subjectivity and Australian Convict Autobiographies, 1788-1899', or 'The Sway of Chance in Eighteenth Century England'. Of course these dissertations may well use literary texts as examples, but if so, the fictions, dramas, or poems in question are taken to be means to an end – they are the windows through which we see the world beyond the text, the symptoms of particular cultural desires, drives, anxieties, or prejudices. Thus, the classical and medieval rhetorical triad – *docere, delectare, movere* (to teach, to delight, to move) – a triad operative for centuries – has been reduced to a single one: the teaching function. Not surprisingly, then, the governing paradigm for so-called literary study is now taken from anthropology and history, as the emphasis on dates indicates. As a test case, consider three titles of current fellowship projects at the National Humanities Center in Chapel Hill:

1. Traveling Philosophers: The Constitution of a Pragmatist International Network, 1890-1920

2. Stages of transition: Performing South Africa's Truth Commission

3. Lollard Affect and the Contestation of Holiness, 1370-1550

I invite you to guess from which departments these project statements emerge? Philosophy, Political Science, Religious Studies, in that order? No: the first, 'Traveling Philosophers', is by a historian, the second, on South Africa's Truth Commission, by a professor of theatre, and the third on the Lollard contestation of holiness by an English professor.

For many of us, this blurring of boundaries has been regarded as a healthy sign, a marker of our new found *interdisciplinarity*. Perhaps. But, whatever the 'inter' in the topics listed above, there is one discipline that is conspicuously absent, and that discipline is what the Greeks called *Poetike*, the discipline of Poetics. True, the South African Truth Commission may be better understood when we examine its workings as a form of theatre, and the meaning of "holiness" for the followers of John Wycliff may well have a strong rhetorical component. But in these and related cases, the 'literary,' if it matters at all, is always secondary; it has at best an instrumental value. Accordingly, it would be more accurate to call the predominant activity of contemporary 'literary' scholars *other*-disciplinary rather than *inter*-disciplinary.

Why *is* the 'merely' literary so suspect today? There can be no easy answer to this question, but perhaps the first thing to acknowledge is that it is by no means a new one. Consider, for instance, the argument of Plato's *Ion*. This early dialogue, written sometime in the first decade of the 4th century BCE, is set in Athens: it presents Socrates in conversation with the rhapsode Ion, who has just returned from Epidaurus, where he has won first prize at a festival in honor of Asclepius. A *rhapsode* was part performance artist, part literary critic; he gave public recitations, followed by critical commentaries upon them and drew large audiences. Ostensibly Ion, whose specialty was Homer, drew 20,000 people at Epidaurus; he wore a golden crown and received handsome payment.

Socrates begins by positing that surely a *rhapsode* "must comprehend the utterances of the poet [in question], for the *rhapsode* must become an interpreter of the poet's thought [*dianoia*] for those who listen."[vi] How is it,

---

vi. Plato, *Ion*, trans. Lane Cooper, *The Collected Dialogues of Plato*, ed. Edith Hamilton and Huntington Cairns (Princeton: Princeton University Press, Bollingen Series LXXI, 1961), 216-28. I refer, as is conventional, to the marginal sigla, here §530, of the standard Greek edition. *The Republic*, trans. Paul Shorey is cited from the same Bollingen edition.

he wonders, that Ion is "skilled in Homer, but not in Hesiod or the other poets"? After all, Socrates suggests, don't all the poets talk about war, about the relations of men, good and bad, the birth of gods and heroes, and so on? Ion has no answer: he only knows that Hesiod puts him to sleep whereas he adores Homer. To which Socrates responds:

> The riddle is not hard to solve, my friend. Now, it is plain to everyone that not from art and knowledge [*ouk techne kai episteme*] comes your power concerning Homer. If it were *techne* [art, method] that gave you power, then you could speak about all the other poets as well. (532c)

Indeed, Socrates concludes, it is not through art [*ouk en technes*] but through divine inspiration [*en-theos*], through being taken out of his senses [*ekplexis*] that the *rhapsode* can recite and comment on Homer (533, 35): he is, in fact, a second-order or lesser poet, no more than a middleman passing along the Homeric aura. Thus, in the rest of the dialogue, Socrates 'proves' that Ion knows less about charioteering than any charioteer and hence cannot properly talk about athletic contests in Homer, and that the same thing is true for the physician, the diviner, and the fisherman. Defensively, Ion finally responds that what he does know is "The kind of thing [...] that man would say, and a woman would say, and a slave and free man, a subject and a ruler – the suitable thing, for each" (540b). This is in fact the doctrine of *to prepon* ["fitness"], which will become central in Aristotle's *Poetics*. But here Socrates pooh-poohs the idea and concludes that there is no such thing as an art and science of poetry, no such thing, in other words, as literary criticism.

Logically speaking, this conclusion has always been difficult to counter. Whereas economists or physicists, geologists or climatologists, physicians and lawyers, must master a body of knowledge before they can even think of being licensed to practice, we literary scholars, it is tacitly assumed, have no definable expertise. Is it a question of having mastered the history of English literature from Beowulf to the present? Certainly, in the United States this is no longer a requirement: we are, after all, not British, and besides downplaying American literature, the EngLit requirement would not include Anglophone literature from Australia and Africa, from the Caribbean and Canada. The same argument applies in the case of French or German or Spanish literature.

Is our expertise, then, in literary theory? For a brief moment in the sixties and seventies, this seemed to be the case: 'everyone' had to know their

Marx and Freud, their Benjamin and Adorno, their Foucault and Derrida, their Lacan and Kristeva. But increasingly, this Eurocentric theory has come to seem less than adequate in dealing with the growing body of minority, transnational and postcolonial literature, and so Poststructuralist theory is being replaced by critical race studies and related models, but so eclectic have the categories become that in most colleges and universities there is now no theory requirement at all.

The third traditional role of literary studies – evaluation – is currently dismissed as largely anachronistic. Value is generally understood as a cultural product: what we value depends on our race, class, gender, and ethnicity, our prior educational experience, our age, and so on. There are no universally 'great' works, no individual geniuses. True, Shakespeare continues, somewhat grudgingly, to be taught and studied everywhere, but I have heard prominent scholars say this is not because the author William Shakespeare wrote such unique and wonderful plays, plays to which we feel everyone should be exposed, but because Shakespeare is now a code word for a giant culture industry and historical complex: a carrier of socio-political meanings too influential to ignore.

Given these aporias of literary study, perhaps, administrators are beginning to argue, English departments should concentrate on the study of composition and rhetoric, disciplines that really do teach students things they need to know, and on language learning, so important in business, professional life, and especially for those in government or with government contracts. Indeed, as you may have heard, the current administration has made a great push to strengthen the role of the 'less-frequently taught' languages – Arabic, Farsi, Chinese, and so on – in the curriculum.

Still, I wonder how many of us, no matter how culturally and politically oriented our own particular research may be, would be satisfied with the elimination of literary study from the curriculum? Again, Plato provides us with an understanding of the conundrum. It is the Plato of the *Republic* who argues that the future Guardians of the State should not be exposed to poetry, precisely because the poetic is too appealing, too seductive, too dangerous, too prone to the telling of powerful "lies" about gods and mortals. When, for example the *Iliad* portrays Achilles, the son of a goddess, as "'lying now on his side, and then again on his back, and again on his face,' and then rising up and 'drifting distraught on the shore of the waste unharvested ocean . . . weeping and lamenting'" (388 b), a bad example is set for young people. Heroes do not behave that way, or do they? "We will beg Homer," Socrates says famously, "not to be angry if we cancel those and all similar passages, not that they are not poetic and pleasing to most hearers, but because *the more poetic they are, the less are they suited to the ears of boys and men* who are destined to be free and to be more afraid of slavery than of death" (387b). And in Book X, poetry is classified as an imitation twice removed from the realm of truth (the passage from the Idea of the chair, to the actual chair, and the image of a chair) and hence:

> We can admit no poetry into our city save only hymns to the gods and the praises of good men. For if you grant admission to the honeyed Muse in lyric or epic, pleasure and pain will be the lords of your city instead of law and that which shall from time to time have approved itself to the general reason as the best. (607a)

But how and why does the art called poetry exert such a magic spell? If it brings us no closer to the true or the good (the exemplary case of the latter is the Nazi love of Goethe and Beethoven), how can it be judged powerful enough to be dangerous, to transform the lives of those it touches? Again, why do so many people want to *be* poets, novelists, artists, composers, even as others, like many of us here tonight, want to be *rhapsodes*?

Plato himself, we should note, did not practice the separation between poetry and philosophy he preaches: he knew very well that although the study of literature is not a science, there are nevertheless many local truths to be articulated. In Book III of the *Republic,* for example, he lays out the crucial voice distinctions, foundational for all subsequent theorists, between the basic literary modes – lyric, narrative, dramatic – and in the *Phaedrus*, he provides us with a fascinating discussion of poetic etymology vis-à-vis the role sound and the material word play in specific poetic instances. It was left to Aristotle to draw out the implications of Plato's analysis in Chapter IX of the *Poetics*:

> A poet's object is not to tell what actually happened but what could and would happen either probably or inevitably. The difference between a historian and a poet is not that one writes in prose and the other in verse... The real difference is this, that one tells what happened the other what might happen. For this reason poetry is something more philosophical and serious [*philosophoteron kai spoudaioteron*] than history, because poetry tends to give general truths while history gives particular facts.[vii]

vii. Aristotle, *The Poetics,* trans. W. Hamilton Fyfe (Cambridge: Harvard University Press, Loeb Classics, 1960), 1453b.

Thus (Chapter XXIV), "What is convincing though impossible should always be preferred to what is possible and unconvincing" (1460a). And in XXV "the standard of what is correct is not the same in the art of poetry as it is in the art of social conduct" (1460b).

This last sentence is considered one of the defining classical statements of theory and takes us all the way to Wittgenstein's precept "Do not forget that a poem, although it is composed in the language of information, is not used in the language-game of giving information."[viii] At the same time, these precepts have always been questioned, in our day, for example, by Stanley Fish, whose *Is There a Text in this Class?* (1980), argues that, logically speaking, there is, in fact, no absolute distinction between ordinary and poetic language. There are always exceptions. Again, Aristotle's insistence that the end of tragedy (or epic) is to produce *pleasure*, its own particular kind of pleasure, has been contested, never more loudly than in recent decades. Historians, poststructuralist theory has insisted, don't tell the truth any more than do the poets; their writing – think of Gibbon – can be just as artistically structured as that of a novel, and historical writing is, in any case, hardly disinterested. Or again – to take the other side – although poets don't tell "what happened" in the simple way Aristotle puts it, of course their representations, once we know how to decode them, tell us everything about such matters as power relations, psychological identities, and class structures in the period and culture that has generated the text in question. Indeed, if, as Foucault has taught us, all we have are representations rather than realities, of course we must read those representations as cultural indices.

Still, once the pendulum has swung as far as it has in its equation of *mimesis* and *diegesis*, *representation* and *reference*, between mimesis and dianoia, it inevitably begins to move the other way. It happened in the late sixteenth century in Sidney's eloquent *Defense of Poesy*, written in response to Stephen Gosson's Puritan pamphlet *The School of Abuse* (1579). Gosson, a recent Oxford graduate and acquaintance of Sydney's, used elaborate Euphuistic mannerisms to produce an attack on lyric poets, dramatists, and writers of epic as "caterpillars of the Commonwealth," drones who produce work that is trivial and corrupt. Sidney, to whom *The School of Abuse* was (ironically?) dedicated, rose to the challenge: in his *Defense*, he makes an inspiring case for "Poesie" as "an arte of imitation, for so Aristotle termeth it in his word *Mimesis*, that is to say, a representing, counterfetting, a figuring forth: to speak metaphorically, a speaking picture: with the end, to teach and to delight."[ix]

viii. Ludwig Wittgenstein, *Zettel*, ed. G. E. M. Anscombe and G. H. von Wright, trans. G. E. M. Anscombe (Berkeley: University of California Press, 1967), §160.
ix. Philip Sidney, *A Defense of Poesy*, ed. Jan A. Van Dorsten (New York: Oxford, 1966), 25.

Here the Aristotelian and Horatian concepts of *poiesis* come together in what was to be the established view of poetry for centuries to come. Gosson's attack on the poet as corrupter of youth, an idea no doubt derived from Plato, is famously sidestepped by Sidney's contention that "The poet nothing affirmeth, and therefore never lieth" (52). For Sidney, the poet is above all a *maker* [*poietes*], the creator of an invented world, superior to our own. It was a doctrine revived by the Romantics and again by the Modernists, for example Wallace Stevens, who insisted in 'The Noble Rider and the Sound of Words', written on the eve of World War II, that "A possible poet must be a poet capable of resisting or evading the pressure of the reality of this last degree [of violence]." And a few pages later: "What makes the poet the potent figure that he is, or was, or ought to be, is that he creates the world to which we turn incessantly and without knowing it [...] he gives to life the supreme fictions without which we are unable to conceive of it."[x] If poetry is the "supreme fiction," or in Pound's more practical terms, "News that stays news," then the study of literature cannot assign to the texts in question a merely instrumental value, a tool to be used to get at the problems of ethnic identity or cultural change. As Adorno put it, "The greatness of works of art [...] consists solely in the fact that they give voice to what ideology hides."[xi]

A spectre is haunting the academy, the spectre of literature. Just this year, 2006, Terry Eagleton, perhaps best known for such theory primers as *Literary Theory: An Introduction* (1983) and *The Ideology of the Aesthetic* (1990), has published a book called *How to Read a Poem*. Eagleton's opening chapter, "The Functions of Criticism," begins as follows:

> I first thought of writing this book when I realized that hardly any of the students of literature I encountered these days practiced what I myself had been trained to regard as literary criticism. Like thatching or clog dancing, literary criticism seems to be something of a dying art.[xii]

It is not, Eagleton goes on to say, that students don't read texts closely. "Close reading is not the issue. The question is not how tenaciously you cling to the text, but what you are in search of when you do so." Students today, he worries, are only taught "content analysis":

x. Wallace Stevens, 'The Noble Rider and the Sound of Words' (1942), in Stevens, *The Necessary Angel: Essays on Reality and the Imagination* (New York: Random House: Vintage Books, 1965), 27, 33.
xi. Theodor W. Adorno, 'On Lyric Poetry and Society' (1957), in *Notes to Literature*, Vol. 1, ed. Rolf Tiedemann, trans. Shierry Weber Nicholsen (New York: Columbia University Press, 1974), 39.
xii. Terry Eagleton, *How to Read a Poem* (Oxford: Blackwell, 2007), 1.

They give accounts of works of literature which describe what is going on in them, perhaps with a few evaluative comments thrown in. To adapt a technical distinction from linguistics, they treat the poem as *language* but not as *discourse*. 'Discourse' [...] means attending to language in all if its material density, whereas most approaches to poetic language tend to disembody it. [...] It would be hard to figure out, just by reading most of these content analyses, that they were supposed to be about poems or novels rather than about some real-life happening. What gets left out is the *literariness* of the work [...] they treat the poem as though its author chose for some eccentric reason to write out his or her views on warfare or sexuality in lines which do not reach to the end of the page. Maybe the computer got stuck. (2-3)

I think this is right on the mark. I have heard graduate students discuss the vagaries of romantic self-consciousness in Shelley's 'Ode to the West Wind' who cannot tell you what an ode is, what apostrophe is, or why (much less how) this one is written in terza rima. But whose fault is this? Not that of theory, for consider – and I concur – the excellent theorists, from Roman Jakobson and William Empson to Hélène Cixous and Julia Kristeva who have written close critical commentary on particular poems (2). Rather, Eagleton posits, the culprit is "a specific way of life." "What threatens to scupper verbal sensitivity," according to Eagleton, "is the depthless, commodified, instantly legible world of advanced capitalism, with its unscrupulous way with signs, computerized communication and glossy packaging of 'experience'." Indeed, "what is at peril on our planet is *experience itself*" (17).

It sounds ominous: Eagleton's is only the latest in a series of books and articles that posit "the death of literature" (see, for example, William Marx's *La Mort de la littérature* of 2006) and bemoan the inability of the young to read any piece of prose (much less poetry) longer than a few pages. But my own experience has been quite otherwise. Who, for starters, is to say what constitutes an "experience" and that some people are incapable of having one? And does "late capitalism" really "scupper" that "sensitivity" to poetic language, a sensitivity that was presumably intact during capitalism's earlier, less global stages? On the contrary: it is my hunch that the "computerized communication" Eagleton dismisses so nostalgically is precisely the medium that is generating a renewed interest in poetry as well as in literary studies: witness the intense debate on particular poetic issues on the internet. To come back to Beckett for a moment, the Centennial events I spoke of earlier are posted, along with major Beckett texts, commentaries, reviews, and visual sources, on an anonymous site called *Samuel Beckett: Resources and Links* (http://samuel-beckett.net/). This and other Beckett sites receive thousands of hits.

Indeed, the trickle-down effect of such internet activity is beginning to transform the university classroom Eagleton speaks of so sadly. On *PennSound* (http://www.writing.upenn.edu/pennsound/), the site co-founded in January 2005 by Charles Bernstein and Al Filreis at the University of Pennsylvania's CPCW (Center for Programs in Contemporary Writing), you may, with the click of a finger, hear Gertrude Stein read her tongue-in-cheek homage poem to T. S. Eliot called 'The Fifteenth of November' (1924), or George Oppen read, in his quiet, sometimes breaking voice, his long serial poem 'Of Being Numerous' (1968), or even Vladimir Mayakovsky's *Ez ulitsi v ulitsu* ('From Street to Street'), read by the poet's mistress Lili Brik. The unique feature of *PennSound* is that one needn't hear complete recordings of this or that poet but can choose precisely the poem one wants to access. Each poet, moreover, has his or her own page, giving us titles, sources, length of playing time, and, in the case of Russian or other foreign languages, the written text in the original and translation.

It goes without saying that these tools revolutionize the poetry classroom. Or again, at Kenneth Goldsmith's *Ubu Web* (http://www.ubu.com/), which covers experimental writing – sound poetry, concrete poetry, performance – from Apollinaire and Marinetti to the present – you can now also see such art films as Duchamp's *Anaemic Cinema* and Robert Smithson's *Spiral Jetty*. As little as ten years ago, an instructor friend, who wanted to show Smithson's film to her students in a course on language in visual art, had to pay a large sum for the rental of the film print, and the copy took weeks to arrive. Now it is right there for anyone with a web browser to access. Thousands of writers, artists, students, professors, and just plain interested parties around the world are accessing the esoteric websites and blogs in question and reading or listening to difficult avant-garde texts. Then, too, via *PennSound*, students in New Zealand or Santiago can hear Penn's John Richetti reading Pope's 'Rape of the Lock' or David Wallace reading Chaucer's *Pardoner's Tale*, which is, in its turn, parodied in Caroline Bergvall's contemporary riff on Chaucer, also online.

But – I am often asked – won't this digi-mania marginalize *The Book* even more completely? Will anyone read, say, an entire Victorian novel when one can cruise the net, accessing sound bytes from *Bleak House* or synopses of *Wuthering Heights*? Here a little anecdote, this time from popular culture, might be apposite.

Many of you will recall last year's brouhaha in response to Oprah

Winfrey's September 2005 Book Club selection of *A Million Little Pieces*, a memoir of addiction and recovery by a young Hollywood screenwriter named James Frey. The previous year, Oprah had been justly praised for choosing as selections such classics as *Anna Karenina* and three Faulkner novels: *The Sound and the Fury*, *As I Lay Dying*, and *Light in August*. Tolstoy's novel, which had been selling about 12,000 copies a year in the new Penguin translation of Richard Pevear and Larissa Volokhonsky (2001), jumped, thanks to Oprah, to 900,000 in 2004.[xiii] But these sales figures – spectacular as they are for a classic – were nothing compared to those of Oprah's next selection, *A Million Little Pieces*, which had sold 1.77 million copies in four months, when, in January 2006, it was exposed by *The Smoking Gun* website as being largely a fabrication.[xiv] The author, it seems, had invented many of the books' sordid and sensational incidents. On national television, Oprah now confronted Frey, telling him that he had "betrayed millions of readers," and that she herself had been "duped." In a rare show of anger, she accused Doubleday (now a Random House imprint), the memoir's publisher, of having failed to employ the proper fact-checkers, and, after much legal wrangling, Doubleday agreed to add a disclaimer to all subsequent copies of the book – a disclaimer in which James Frey admitted that he had "embellished" the story, but that the basic purpose of the book – originally written as a novel – had not appreciably been altered. "Ultimately," he protests, "it's a story, and one that I could not have written without having lived the life I've lived."[xv]

This is a cautionary tale, but not for those who want to learn about substance abuse and recovery. Frey's 'novel' had been turned down by seventeen publishers before being accepted by Doubleday's Nan Talese, provided the author would revise it as a memoir.[xvi] The decision to publish *A Million Little Pieces* in its new form was based, of course, on a single consideration – a the bottom line: if Oprah was 'duped', she was duped primarily by Frey's publisher. How, for example, could fact-checkers, who are, after all, office employees, have done the detective work performed, ironically, not by anyone in the publishing world, but by the website *The*

xiii. See Anna Malpas, 'Oprah's Pick', *Context*, 25 June 2004
http://context.themoscowtimes.com/stories/2004/06/25/101.html
xiv. See 'The Man Who Conned Oprah', *The Smoking Gun*
http://www.thesmokinggun.com/archive/0104061jamesfrey1.htm, (8 January 2006); and cf.
Edward Wyatt, 'Oprah Calls Defense of Author "a Mistake"', *New York Times,* 26 January 2006
http://www.nytimes.com/2006/01/26/books/26cnd-oprah.html/
xv. James Frey, 'A Note to the Reader'
http://www.randomhouse.com/trade/publicity/pdfs/AMLP020106.pdf
xvi. See *The Smoking Gun*, 8 January 2006.

Smoking Gun, which used interviews with law enforcement personnel, police reports, and court records to come to its well documented conclusions?

The book's alleged "authenticity," which so enchanted Oprah that she couldn't put it down, thus raises large issues about the probity of commercial publishers and the power of the internet to act as whistle blower. More important: it raises those basic literary questions I posed earlier. What is the relation of truth to fiction? Can a memoir invent or embellish incidents and still be 'true' to the author's experience? Rousseau certainly thought so as did the Goethe of *Dichtung und Wahrheit* or the Elias Canetti of *The Tongue Set Free*. Is Sylvia Plath's *The Bell Jar* a novel or a memoir? And what about *The Autobiography of Malcolm X*, subtitled "as told to Alex Haley"? To cite Aristotle once more, "What is convincing though impossible should always be preferred to what is possible and unconvincing".

A related question – and here we turn to literary history – has to do with genre and convention. To study the nature of narrative is to come to *A Million Little Pieces* with a horizon of expectations rather different from that of Oprah and her core readership. For what is *A Million Little Pieces* but an up-to-date, steamy version of the familiar addiction-recovery paradigm found in such classics as De Quincey's *Confessions of an English Opium Eater* or Baudelaire's *Le Vin et le Hashish*, or, closer to home, William Burroughs's *Junky* (1953), the ultimate addiction narrative. Indeed, the to hell-and-back curve of Frey's "memoir" is the familiar curve of conversion narratives, beginning with the dramatic opening of Chapter III of Augustine's *Confessions*: "To Carthage then I came, where a cauldron of unholy loves sang all about mine ears." And what is probably the greatest to hell-and-back story of all, Dante's *Inferno*, begins, like Frey's, at rock bottom, as the "I" narrator finds himself in a "dark forest," with the *via diritta* or way out wholly blocked to him.

Who, then, is being duped here, and how? You may recall that in 2004 the National Endowment for the Arts issued a report called *Reading at Risk* that concluded ominously, from a survey of respondents who were asked how many "literary" books (novels, poems, and plays) they had read in the preceding year, that the current cultural "crisis" is such that "literary reading as a leisure activity will virtually disappear in a half century."[xvii] But what is "literary reading" and is such reading confined to books? If, for example, Frey had somehow managed to publish *A Million Little Pieces* as the novel it was meant to be, would reading *this* book count toward the kind of cultural literacy the NEA report takes to be so essential? Is reading fiction, never mind

---

xvii. Dana Gioia (ed.), *Reading at Risk: A Survey of Literary Reading in America* (National Endowment for the Arts, 2004).

what fiction, always preferable to reading an essay like the one from *Smoking Gun* on line? And what about the values of book production? When Penguin, one of the most distinguished publishers, brought out the Pevear translation of *Anna Karenina* in 2001, its cover depicted the nude knees of a woman, with a bouquet of flowers held by her right hand, between the knees. This was the edition picked up by the Oprah Book Club, the edition that sold 900,000 copies. *Anna Karenina*, anyone?

Where, then, do we as teachers of language and literature come in? If we choose to assign Tolstoy's great novel in a given course, as I hope many of us will, we should begin with some large and basic literary questions. First theory: what *is* a novel and how does its fictionality relate to truth. Levin, the male hero of *Anna*, although one wouldn't know this from the Penguin cover or the publicity machine, was, after all, based closely on Tolstoy himself, and so questions of truth and 'reality' are particularly pressing in the case of this so-called 'realistic' novel. What is the narrative's point of view, and how does language work in articulating it? Why do readers, more than a hundred years after its publication, continue to be enthralled by *Anna Karenina* when presumably *A Million Little Pieces* will have vanished from literary and cultural memory by next year? What, in short, makes a novel News that Stays News?

Then literary history and geography: where do we place this particular novel in the larger literary field? *Anna Karenina*'s adultery story is, in one sense, as old as the hills – think of Clytemnestra's betrayal of Agamemnon – and in another both historically based in late nineteenth-century bourgeois culture and peculiar to Russian society in the wake of the emancipation of the serfs and in the light of the coming revolution. And finally, literary criticism which can only work if we read very closely and evaluatively. *Anna* is a great test case because it seems at one level to be so ordinary, its narrative more or less writing itself. No elaborate fictional devices like flashbacks and multiple narrators, very little metaphor, allusion, or stylization. And yet nothing is stranger than this particular 'ordinariness', beginning with the opening sentence, "Happy families are all alike; each unhappy family is unhappy in its own way." This sentence, incidentally, which I cite from Aylmer Maude's translation, is rendered slightly differently by Richard Pevear: "All happy families are alike, each is unhappy in its own way." If we could read the novel in Russian – and we should encourage as much study of literature in its original language as possible – we would obviously be in a better position to judge.

How, in any case, does this proverbial sentence function? Is the distinction Tolstoy's? The omniscient narrator's? The perspective of Stiva or

Dolly Oblonsky, whose broken marriage begins this story? That of the common wisdom of Tolstoy's day? Or is this a sentence as sardonic as Jane Austen's "It is a truth universally acknowledged..."? By the time we finish *Anna*, we have learned that even the "happiest" families like Levin and Kitty's, are not really happy at all. You will recall that in one of the novel's last chapters, when Levin is living "happily" in the country with his adored Kitty and their new baby, the narrator tells us that "though he was a happy and healthy family man, Levin was several times so near to suicide that he hid a cord he had lest he should hang himself, and he feared to carry a gun lest he should shoot himself."[xviii] But he does not hang himself any more than Gogo or Didi hang themselves from that lone leafless tree in *Godot*, and it would be a fascinating project to determine how these so utterly unlike hanging scenes might relate to one another. In Tolstoy's world, a world not nearly as dark as Beckett's, humor is in very short supply, and Levin cannot shake off his anxieties by laughing at himself. Why is that?

Contemplating such questions, those of us who teach literature may come to see that we have a lot more *expertise* than we think we have. It is time to trust the literary instinct that brought us to this field in the first place and to recognize that, rather than lusting after those other disciplines that seem so exotic primarily because we don't really practise them, what we need is more theoretical, historical, and critical training in our own discipline. *Rhapsodes*, it turns out, can and should serve a real function in our oral, print and digital culture. Supply and demand, or should I say, surveying the Beckett field of 2006, demand and supply: the time is fast coming, I believe, when this basic law must and will operate in our favour.

---

xviii. Leo Tolstoy, *Anna Karenina*, trans. Aylmer Maude, ed. George Gibian (New York: Norton Critical Edition, 1995), 714.

Marjorie Perloff is Professor Emeritus of English Literature at Stamford University. Among the best-known of her critical works are *Wittgenstein's Ladder: Poetic Language and the Strangeness of the Ordinary* (1996) and *Poetry On and Off the Page: Essays for Emergent Occasions* (1998).

Lyric and *Razo*:
Activism and the Poet

JOHN KINSELLA

An essay on activism and poetry is by necessity a personal one. For me, environmentalism, for want of a better word, is what I do in life and in writing. However, long ago I differentiated between polemic and open-endedness, between rhetoric and, if one likes, the lyric impulse. Rarely does one write a poem of pure anything; but ultimately, though not exclusively, I try to keep the balance towards the open-ended lyric rather than propagandist rhetoric. Although I can get mighty pissed off and even write poems with subtitles like 'a poem of abuse'; but I try to undo my own sincerity and zeal with irony and/or figurative tugs of the carpet from beneath the certainty of my 'feet'. A poem in which language is not the prime generator is no poem at all for me. What's more, such a poem is a hell of a lot less effective as activism. If the reader has to work at the poem, s/he is more likely to think about the issues being explored, struggled with. Poetry should be a struggle.

I seem to be embroiled in an endless debate about the whys and wherefores of political poetry. Arguments that the poem is political regardless of intent because of how and where it is read, and the cultural implications of language selection and usage, make it a very open debate. But, in essence, the debate revolves more around poems as activism: the poem working for a specific political end, most often a form of change or correction. On activist discussion groups, many participants have an inclination for poetry, and poetry and 'the arts' in general become an extension of political statement. Borrowing and usage of 'found' texts and images, manipulating visual and textual representations from mainstream culture, are commonplace. The familiar expression 'culture jamming' denotes an undermining of the status quo through manipulation of 'problematical' images that have become all too readily accepted. One 'poem' on an activist discussion list that recently annoyed me and my partner Tracy involved the use of a woman with her mouth open provocatively, probably taken from a porn site, with a snappy, disposable and suitably ironic political caption beneath. In essence, we as viewers are supposed to deconstruct our own sense of viewing, to challenge the misogynistic and fetishised use of the female. In reality, we argue, one has one's cake and eats it too. The woman in the image is still exploited, and our awareness is merely... well, lip service. This is poetry as failed activism to my mind.

A recent discussion with an anarchist activist friend of mine involved differentiating our respective anarchisms. He termed his 'aesthetic', and mine 'moral'. It's an interesting distinction, though no differentiations are decisive. When I write an 'activist poem', it is for a moral purpose, but the reason I select poetry as a form of expression is as much because of the constraints as of the freedoms of the 'genre' (I don't like categories!). But then, the most polemical poems (and thus the most ineffective outside their immediate moment/action, I'd argue), often use absorbable sing-song and banal rhythms and strict rhyming patterns: these are 'aids to memory', mnemonic devices to allow the message to be carried by word-of-mouth. Oral poetry, sure, but oral poetry resisting the change that comes with slippage, error, and interpolation – I am talking here of the polemical poem that means exactly what it says, serves a specific purpose, and is never intended to grow with the telling. By contrast, when I write an 'activist' poem, I want it to be misinterpreted as much as interpreted, want even something that seems overt to be questionable – at least through that basic and fallible device: irony.

One of the objections to the activist poem is that its range is necessarily narrow. Motivated by an extreme of emotion, it doesn't allow readers themselves to invest a personal scale or chromatics of emotion. I challenge this: an activist poem should motivate investigation, not tell readers what to think. Data are data, as subjective as the presentation might be. Data can find their way into the poem, but the figurative medium mediates our response to 'fact'. Fact can, in fact, become misdirection, and certainly misprision.

This essay is also really a long *razo* for a life of writing poetry. In the superb volume *Razos and Troubadour Songs* (tr. William E. Burgwinkle, Volume 71, Series B, Garland Library of Medieval Literature, New York and London, 1990), the introduction opens with a paragraph useful to our intent here to quote in full:

> The usage of the Occitan word *razo* within the body of thirteenth- and fourteenth-century texts collected in this volume reveals how fully medieval authors came to exploit the semantic richness of the word's Latin model, *ratione(m)*. The most generalized and reductive definition, and the one which came in time to define a literary genre, is this: introduction, explanation, reasoned commentary, subject matter, background, gloss. Indeed, we do find that all the short prose

texts collected here clearly serve in one way or another an introductory function in relation to the songs with which they are paired. Referring to, and citing, specific lyric texts composed by troubadours of Southern France, Northern Italy and Spain, the author claims to provide an explanation for why a particular poet composed a particular song or songs at the moment that he or she did. At the same time, he does not treat the song in a vacuum; rather, by adopting a uniform rhetorical practice and vocabulary, he relates the song to a larger social and literary phenomenon: the composition and exchange of vernacular songs of praise in the Southern French courts. (xvii)

While many might argue that prose would be a more effective tool for the activist – that is more to the point, and more direct – I would argue differently. However, prose might form an important prelude, even component, of poetry. Be it Dante's *La Vita Nuova*, or the *razos* written to accompany troubadour songs, explication is an active and integral part of poetry. Whether in the glosses of 'The Rime of the Ancient Mariner', or the prose 'responses' within the haibun, prose becomes a counterpoint. This prose doesn't have to 'explain' a poem – in fact, who really wants a poem explained? – but it can interact and hence enrich, and highlight or offset the poem. A bit like a frame around a painting, or the space around a sculpture. This essay, then, is an auto-*razo* to an activist poetics.

Before I take a public action – write a letter of complaint, give a public lecture, attend a protest – I inevitably write a poem on the subject. Poems usually follow the action too. And might continue to do so long after the event or issue has passed, even if there's been a negative outcome (a forest block has been logged/mined/cleared, for example). The writing of poems becomes part of a mantra of witness and empowerment. Often, poems form a visceral and literal part of a protest. In what follows I am going to explore two recent activist issues, of very different but still related natures. I will then to chart their appearance and digressions in poetry. Basically, the issues are:

1. Visiting a forest protest site in the Arcadia jarrah forest in the south-west of Australia to lend support to activists.
2. Involvement in a recent Indymedia discussion/protest against the use of violence by activists at the G20 conference held recently in Melbourne.

Each of these 'actions' involved the writing of prose and poetry.

The net, especially Indymedia, became my source of information regarding logging activities in Arcadia Forest. This regrowth jarrah block located near the Wellington Dam catchment, not far from Collie (a coal mining town in Western Australia), is contentious for a number of reasons. First, it's native forest; second, the regrowth since the 1930s has been considerable, and it is a substantial forest of jarrah, marri, with thick undergrowth (snottygobble etc), and finally, it forms a considerable/integral part of the extremely rare and critically endangered habitat of the marsupial land quokka (the quokka is also found on the island of Rottnest, which roughly translates into 'rats' nest', an allusion to quokkas).

Together with an old anarchist friend of mine, I visited the protest camp that had been moved on by police from its original site within the logging area. The preceding days had seen a lot of 'locking on' activities: the use of dragons (concrete and metal anchors, in essence – with arms literally concreted and welded into large objects so the police and loggers can't move protesters without the risk of injury to those protesters – they are usually defeated, however, with an array of cutting equipment), climbing trees (and roping oneself to the trunk/branches), and lying in front of bulldozers, chaining oneself to machines, etc. These direct actions had had little effect. The best such protesters can hope for is intense media interest, and maybe delaying tactics, with the possibility that other forms of protest will prove effective before the damage is done.

Visiting the Arcadia Forest protest campsite convinced me that a holistic plan of action is the only way, a plan to beat the loggers at their own game. I have attended many such protests, and have grown increasingly frustrated with these activities. The government and the companies involved always contradict their own rules: entering dieback areas (dieback is *Phytophthora cinnamomi*, a fungus/pathogen that attacks the roots of trees – it is spread by movement of people and vehicles through the forest), making use of streams, crossing boundaries. Thus I have argued that a legal and written (and photographed) approach/agenda, to highlight the rule-breaking, is essential. Recent legal challenges (by Dr Bob Brown in Tasmania) in terms of protected flora and fauna, have been effective, and I have been told by environmental lawyers that this approach is viable. So I sent this letter to protest organisers:

Hi…

I think what we need to do is prepare some kind of doc of

aims in point form. e.g.

1. To preserve native forests – old growth and previously logged forests. To preserve and protect the wildlife and vegetation therein.
2. To minimise disruptions to native forests. To encourage alternative ways of viewing the intense uniqueness and splendour of these places.
3. To encourage the planting of trees on already (!) cleared land for use as 'timber products'.
4. To establish a fund to be used to defend native forests in court – i.e. through legal avenues.
5. This fund to be used to allow preservation activities to be pursued without the fear that government and private companies can act with impunity because they know those opposed to these activities have no resources to go to court. Very often, loggers and miners and pastoralists act against the law itself (spreading dieback, polluting water, going outside agreed upon boundaries), and no one can afford to challenge them. There are innumerable examples of this and the perpetrators should be held accountable (under their own – inadequate – rules!). Under various wildlife and environmental legislations, there are strong legal grounds for the cessation of logging and usage of native forests.
6. To establish a pool of interested legal people who are prepared to work for little or nothing.
7. To establish a charity or related status (i.e. creating a position/structure re dealing with donated funds and using them for legal purposes).
8. To actively promote such a fund to interested parties. A clear outline of how the money will be used and how it will be managed is essential and the key to receiving donations.
9. Those we (the group) take legal action against should know that we are financially capable of losing. That's the trick – not that we only hope (expect) to win, but that we can lose and then have enough up our sleeve to appeal and to mount another legal challenge in a different area.

This is just off the top of my head – interested people should feed into such a doc – consensus is essential. Once we have these sorted, I think we should look for donors – and I am very happy to work towards this end.

best,
jk

Now, it might seem there is little to connect this with poetry but, in fact, there's a poetics in this approach. As an anarchist, interaction with legals in this context does not appeal to me, but in the end they are the translators of language to fact in the structures with which one has to deal regarding this matter. 'The Law' takes the kernel of the poem and writes the *razo* that come before it. As a connected action, I took the poems I had written about this issue, and circulated them. I had done the same thing after attending the Ludlow Tuart Forest protest a few years before.

Poetry is an effective way of taking the discussion out of 'interest areas' into a broader discussion. I would argue that the metonymic connection between the trees we exploit for paper, and our writing, is just cause for investigation of source and culpability on behalf of the writer. I gave a workshop a few years ago when two smart teenagers spent their time mocking environmentalism in writing because of this very reason. It's an obvious target, nothing really smart there, but I had to pay them credit for their consistency. The issue, the contradictions, weren't going to go away. Computers accepted (and they too bring their own myriad of environmental issues), paper is the tissue of the writer's body. I was down south last week, checking out plantation timber: native bushland surreptitiously cleared, the use of pesticides and herbicides – the golden dream is not always so golden. It needs vigilance, monitoring, and writing about. What we write with and on are part of the responsibility.

The problems of the plantation timber industry aside, the starting point is the preservation of native forests. Here is a poem written in protest to the logging of jarrah in native forests in Western Australia. It was written prior to the Arcadia protest, but with the same region and actions in mind. The first two lines are taken from the *Love Sonnet* by Zora Cross (Australian poet who wrote largely during the First World War) of the same number:

XXXI.

We must look around upon our children dear,
Living through them, this present and that past;
And this is never more evident

Than when walking through old-growth forest;
The toddler ambling ecstatically the filtered light,
Rough-barked jarrah towering and closely packed,
Birds endemic to that place only
Darting around the undergrowth; his pleasure
Palpable, loggers nowhere nearby,
Though yellow markings on trunks,
Pink ribbon fluttering down the valley,
A 'grammar' of his children's barren landscape;
Denecourt's wild walks take us nowhere here,
A lust for aluminium undoing the propaganda.

There are connections between the naturing of the poem and the naturing of de-natured lives: the European wild walk as entertainment and reconnection with 'lost primeval roots' is played with in relation to the colonisation of 'Australia'. This is a poem that celebrates place, and laments loss, but also tackles language as the generator that makes such colonisation possible and likely, as well as challenging it. Language and activism co-exist tautologically, capable of achieving the same ends, and also of being mere distractions. Activism as an act of mere habit is like uttering clichés without respecting and experiencing the richness of the clichés – their necessity for existence, their different inflections and implications with every use.

I chose this poem, in the context of this essay, for the last line: the jarrah is also cleared for mining bauxite, which is then turned into aluminium. Most of us make use of aluminium, including the locked-on activists: in their dragons, and in cooking their meals around the campfire. The inescapable irony in action becomes the undoing of the poem in language. 'Human kind / cannot bear very much reality.' How many of my essays have quoted this truism of T. S. Eliot's? The following poem was written some time after visiting the Arcadia activist site, but with the future activism outlined above in mind. It is part of my version of Dante's *Paradiso*, in progress at the moment. The allusions are all to Dante's twenty-first canto: the contemplative, the golden ladder, predestination, and the usual condemnation of papal corruption. The ingredients are all there for a piece of activist verse that is also a nature lyric (after all, that's what I basically write), and a piece of metatext:

Canto of Arcadia (Saturn, 21)

She won't smile the smile of incineration.
They won't sing the song of disintegration.
Together sprung, noise music, see-through mirrors.

Locusts spin in flurries. They have begun to fly.
The bobtail out the back is fat. Crow feathers
are strewn over acres. Rings forming

in the bright sky. Their descent is known.
The ladder is propped up against the rainwater
tank – I have to ascend to clear the leaves

from the grille, but she would only have me descend:
precarious, I perch. My ears are giving me hell.
Two days ago we drove down to Arcadia.

Into Arcadia along forestry roads, rutted
by logging trucks filling the quota. The protest
camp with its wire and papier-mâché

quokka. Mainland quokkas ranging the jarrah forest.
Four hundred meter corridor – promised – barely
two hundred. The sacred stream, arterial, filled

and forded. In and out of dieback like humour.
Fifty-year regrowth cradling the undergrowth.
Marri trees less useful to Gunns – horror

company – left as Habitat. Marked H in rings.
Occult emblems glowing out of brown-greens.
Ensconced in the forest, fallacy is sucked

into machinery, police wagons. About the campfire
dreadlocked souls discuss lock-on methods. Concrete
and car bodies and piping and their own impact

on the forest. I am here now, the soul glow still
intense but tremulous. Camp dogs snap at flies –
that's memory, and taking the message out

is what's supposed to happen. To be arrested
is to arrest attention? To believe in something
is better than believing in nothing? Tree by tree.

She won't smile the smile of incineration.
They won't sing the song of disintegration.
Together sprung, noise music, see-through mirrors.

This poem leads a dual life as 'entertainment' to be read in a volume of poetry, and as 'activism', preferably read aloud to both activists and those one is protesting against, in order to provoke discussion and debate over a specific environmental issue. It fits in neither role comfortably; neither do I want it to. It is a hybrid.

Moving on to the second broader issue I outlined earlier – the Indymedia discussion (at Perth and Melbourne sites) about violent action at the G20 summit – 'the poem itself' becomes an integral part of an activist response to an action. After the physicality of some activists at the protest (which I did not personally attend), 'response' is everything.

In a nutshell, a group of masked and hooded activists who called themselves 'Uncitizens of Arterial Bloc' committed acts of violence against police vehicles and barriers, and then defended their actions in a manifesto posted to Indymedia and various activist discussions groups on the net. Their claims of being everyperson, and defence of 'purity' in anti-capitalist motivation, and that their acts of violence were against property and not people, didn't wash with me. The following is an extract from my second posting in response to their communiqué that defended their anonymity and violence:

Non-violence is active resistance

by John Kinsella   2006-11-24 7:58 AM +0800

[...] I believe in the empowerment of direct action non-violent protest. I think that one should stand in front of the bulldozers (yes, and one might be bulldozed – the act of allowing it to happen does engender some degree of violence, but here I differentiate – a passive-positive action, the use of one's body to absorb the violence of the state/business/violent parties, seems a reasonable self-choice to make), but not wreck them (though I think they shouldn't exist in the first place – that is, manufacturing of such machines should cease).

I believe one should gather in protest against G20s – not turn the act into a self-serving carnivale that celebrates nothing other than one's own frustration and need for social subservience to one's peer group. Action is driven by necessity – and that's all there is in the wrongness of the world we live in – necessity for action. To me, the sort of action we take matters. Disabling one f-16 does not stop the state-corporate machine that makes the f-16. The state dissolves when we don't do what it tells us to do. It might well kill me for not doing what it wants me to do, but I certainly won't give it the excuse of violence to achieve this end result for its propaganda outlets.

Someone mentioned (somewhere) the Angry Penguins and 'smash the state' in one sentence – what a joke. The Angry Penguins did nothing of the kind – they were largely 'middle-class' self-serving artists who spent most of their time defending themselves from attacks from the left whilst pointing out that they published 'real' Marxists. Take a look at the copies of the Angry Penguins' magazine – lots of pseudo revolution and very little substance outside cultural discussion.

Nothing can be said without implications – nor written. Context might be vital, but words create their own context as well. Quoting Orwell in any way, for example, undoes itself by the fact that the man was a spy against the left he supposedly supported. Oh, and as a vegan, every day is part of a direct action against the violence of animal abuse – what you choose to eat is at the core of who you are, I think. And who WE are. Self-righteous? Everyone with a strongly held set of opinions is. That's what helps us resist. Every small action we take matters – and that's why the how and why of those actions that take place matter so much. I am not saying that one has to be a vegan to make an act valid – I am simply trying to point out that every action has an implication we often don't see or expect. The decision I made many years ago to renounce violence (against everything) has empowered me to be held accountable in ways I would never have owned up to. I was once a very violent person and it saddens me to have to recognise this. Oh, and getting beaten up by the forces of the state doesn't stop them doing it to the next person. I have seen horrendous things happen in lock-ups in the 80s, and, as a consequence, I feel a need to be as effective as I can in my resistances. Non-violence – apart from being an ontological decision – places me in a position to challenge the state and their corporate buddies far more effectively. Self-righteousness? Probably – but I believe it can work. So, opt out, yes! And participate in refusal. Both.

As can be seen, poetics were never far from my response. In the ways that matter to me, the above is really an ars poetica, *sans* a discussion of lyricism! I cannot quote the responses back, but some were quite ferocious. In essence, their defence of violence was paramount. In the end, we get trapped in our own righteousness regarding an issue, and poetry is the only possible mediating force. It usually brings three reactions: empathy, hostility, or 'I don't get it'/indifference. Most fascinating though, is that even though one clearly has an agenda in posting it, especially if one has taken an overt political position beforehand, the ambiguities of prosody and the figurative bring a bizarre calm to the argument. Now, a straightforward rant or polemical piece would likely achieve the opposite, but the poem as ambiguous mediator, as conduit for a 'new language' of discussion allows movement.

Graphology 639: The violent disguisers

Traumatised by the 'psycho violence'
of NVDAs –
    they'd crash a truck
through police lines
        and grow giddy
   with the spilling
of images.

Comrades, they'd say, Comrades,
            it's just a different
tactic,
    we're all on the same sade (I meant to write 'side'
but am reading Freud's *The Psychopathology of Everyday Life*
so will let the slip stay…)
          of disguise, communiqué,
   uncitizening:

hooded (not veiled)
they'd hook a catchcry,
let the wealthy hatch conspiracies,
for they too get hungry
and have their disabilities.

I was recently asked by the editor of *Stylus Poetry* magazine: 'Does writing poetry influence your other writing in regard to approach or technique?' I answered:

> I have always been interested in the blurring of genres. I attempt to operate in a liminal zone, and think that it's pretty hard to leave this liminal zone even if one wishes. There are no categories – only flow and hesitation.

And that seems to be what happens when the non-propagandist (I like to think – though this is all relative and subjective) activist poem – not a contradiction! – is deployed by way of 'answer' and response.

In *The Ecology of Freedom: the emergence and dissolution of hierarchy* (Black Rose Books, Montreal/New York, 1991, rev. ed.), Murray Bookchin laments our contemporary inability "to sense the wealth of subjectivity inherent in ourselves..." (279). The poem morphs the argument because it connects physicality with mental activity, flesh with emotion. A poem is an extension of the body: of self, of community, of body politic. When I write an 'activist' poem, it is not a matter of getting on a soapbox, but of placing my body in the line of discussion.

I heard a wonderful segment on national radio this morning about a nudist (naturist) colony open day in Canberra. The spokesman said that after a while, everybody there basically forgot they (and others) were nude. I wondered, then what's the point? But there is a point there: one can enjoy the 'freedom' of the body, and the enclosures of social discourse. For social discourse is never free, and the manners that mediate our interactions are just a degree removed. Unclothed, sure, but to stare at each other's bared genitals would just be downright rude and inconsiderate. Thus the poem becomes a set of manners, an acceptable (if sometime difficult to comprehend) code of conduct while laying 'oneself' bare. A few more (prior) lines from Bookchin:

> In summary, human rationality must be seen as a form and a derivative of a broader 'mentality', or subjectivity, that inheres

in nature as a whole – specifically, in the long development of increasingly complex forms of substance over the course of natural history. We must be very clear about what this means. Natural history includes a history of mind as well as of physical structures – a history of mind that develops from the seemingly 'passive' interactivity of the inorganic to the highly active cerebral processes of human intellect and volition. This history of what we call 'mind' is cumulatively present not only in the human mind but also in our bodies as a whole, which largely recapitulate the expansive development of life-forms at various neurophysical levels of evolution. (279)

This is a *razo* to a would-be troubadour's song, if ever there was one. Critics have applied Bookchinian readings to my work in the past, and mostly I think these are off the mark, but by allowing more metaphor in his prose than Bookchin (I think) intended, and somewhat decontextualising, the point about interactivity seems to me spot-on as poetic process. One of the problems we encounter when objecting to a linking of poetry and activism, especially in locating the prescriptive 'occasionality' of the poem written because one feels the need to say something, or responding out of emotional 'excess', is that it lacks inspiration or linguistic causality. For many poet-activists for whom writing is a political action – and I would include poets as diverse in their poetics as 'Homer', Shelley, Anjela Duval, Judith Wright, Andrea Brady, Lionel Fogarty, Ouyang Yu, Benjamin Zephaniah and Janet McAdams in this picture – there is a fluidity between the 'passive' and the 'active', and interactivity of body and mind. Interestingly, the body of the activist who risks death to chain him/herself to a bulldozer reverses the equation somewhat, though this is not to deny the 'found' poetry of the moment. Performance is also poetry, and the actions and sounds of struggle emit their own prosody.

Back in my 'bad old days', when I got myself in a difficult physical or mental state, I would recite physics formulas like a mantra, to convince myself I was still alive, and to keep myself in check/calm. V squared = U squared + $2AS$; $V = U + AT$; $S = UT + \frac{1}{2} AT$ squared etc. Tongue-twisters, childish rhymes, whole Yeats poems, all do/did the same trick. In the moment of activism, poetry becomes a binding force. What Bookchin didn't add, of course, is the interstice with spirit/spirituality. But that's a personal angle...

If the troubadour Bertran de Born's songs are often overtly political, it's the less politically referenced troubadour songs that interest me as activist.

In the *razo* to Guiraut de Borneill 242, 51 (B/S, 51) in the Burgwinkle translation, the *razo* writer says of Guiraut: "And while he was there he dreamt a dream, which you will hear about in this song, which says:

> I cannot prevent that to the pain..." (23)

and then the song of the troubadour follows this prose explication, only enriched for the introduction, the context, the curating. The troubadour finishes his song with:

> And toward this end I have made a real effort
> That you might understand every song that I compose (25)

in order that 'his'/the pain of (possibly unrequited...) love and the fact of honour and patronage be clear, much like the activist's intent.

There's not much of a gap between love and activism and the creation of a poem. Apart from protesting against a destruction, the activist poem also attempts to provide moments of the beauty/'good' one is attempting to preserve. That even out of loss, a future positive might be achieved. And this is how the song begins – and I concur with its 'issue', with the association of pain and beauty:

> I cannot prevent my tongue
> From moving to the pain in my tooth
> Or my heart to the new flower
> When I see the branches blossom.
> The songs of birds in love
> Are heard through the woods
> And though I am troubled
> And look unhappy,
> When I see songs and gardens and fields
> I am refreshed and take some comfort. (23)

John Kinsella's latest books include *The New Arcadia* and *Peripheral Light: New and Selected Poems*, both from Norton.

Tunnels and Daylights

ALAN BROWNJOHN

O ut of the tunnel, I am finding it difficult to leave Bond Street station. I have taken the wrong direction at the top of the escalator and end up in some kind of bright, claustrophobic shopping arcade. After finding my way somehow through a bemused crowd lingering in this glitz-and-tack cul-de-sac which has no visible Exit signs, I reach a steep staircase up to a thoroughfare at the top. But it isn't worth it. The daylight up there is Oxford Street.

Five days later, at Chapultepec in Mexico City a square, orange high-speed train drops me on the platform of a low-ceilinged Metro station with *Salida* clearly signed. There is an option of two *salida*s. At the top of the semi-lit stairway of the exit I choose, a turnstile discharges me into an unexpectedly wide vestibule of snack-and-canned-drink counters. In a dark doorway a phosphorescent skeleton offers to develop my films. A little farther on, four corridors of modest, useful shops seem to offer free access to four different streets.

Don't ever suggest meeting anyone here unless you know the station very well. If s/he alights a little later on the same platform and takes the second available *salida*, the exit you didn't choose, the route provides the option of two further corridors before more stairs which lead up into the bright open air without passing through the main vestibule; where, naturally, I choose to wait. Then I count, and realise there appear to be four possible daylights at Chapultepec. I had better try them all, one by one, in case –

The first one I try is a deserted concrete concourse with fierce metal barriers shutting me off from anything resembling an attainable street. There is one single, yard-wide gap in the metal, filled by the open doors of a small green bus. The only release seems to be by catching it, paying about thirty pence, getting off at some normal stop, consulting my vast *Guide to Mexico City* (an 'A–Z' which costs about twelve pounds including its magnifying glass). And walking back at street level. No point in doing that, though. We had arranged to meet at the station. At this moment exactly. I go back to the original vestibule and begin a despairing call, from a fixed Telmex phone to a mobile probably out of credit. Then my companion, who has been trying all the other exits, suddenly taps me on the shoulder.

There is a sunken stone concourse at Hörtorget in Stockholm which I have reached by *Tunnelbana* coming in all the way from the lakeside station at Farsta. I am easily out of the tunnel and crossing this cool, late summer space in mid-September. Its daylight is an open pedestrian square which I can leave by taking wide steps up to Drottningatan; up there I could walk along to August Strindberg's former apartment in one direction or to Gamla Stan, the Old Town, in the other. Today the railings ringing this upper level are a continuous display of placards. And every advertising site on the walls of the tunnel I have just left has displayed the same competing political posters, no other advertising at all.

The quadrennial election is on, the principled passion of Swedish politics in evidence everywhere. In this daylight seven substantial parties are vying for attention with competing posters and clean pinewood huts crammed with activists, leaflets, and gifts of badges and sweets. At a microphone on a platform Jane Fonda is speaking in untranslated English in support of the new Women's Party; which, at the polls on Sunday, doesn't prove as attractive to voters as its leader, the charismatic Gudrun Schyman.

Seven weeks later I am released into a street with four roaring lines of traffic at Bellas Artes. I cross them through a dazzling daylight of street stalls and uniformed bandsmen standing around and talking under crimson umbrellas for protection from the afternoon sun. I blink, and see a little green man on the lights walking a countdown of green seconds: 18, 17, 16. At 16 he walks faster. At 9, he is sprinting. But for all his effort he still changes at 0 into a forbidding little red stationary man. I have only seen him run like this in Mexico City. You never see him even walking in London or Bucharest, though Bucharest allows you the second-by-second countdown of numbers. You see him striding, with regular, sober footsteps, in Stockholm.

The clear dark blue M for *Metro* in Bucharest is unmistakable. So is the T for *Tunnelbana* in Stockholm. The London underground symbol, stolen by a store in Bucharest as its logo (breach of copyright?) is visible in every place where you can tell a station from the shops; which is not true at Bond Street. But the inconspicuous bleached-pink "m" in lower case in Mexico City is frequently hidden behind hoardings and street stalls. Nor does anyone seem able to help me at dusk, not even the smart old woman with the lame leg who must live around here and know the district.

I am half-an-hour completely lost in falling darkness, in a whirl of flickering stall lights and music, nightmarishly stranded in a morass of dodgy back streets. It's as if Angel station in Islington had come out in a Central American version of Chapel Market. And now I am hemmed in by three metal frames wielded by traders dismantling their stalls, and a little scared of being robbed inside a sudden, impromptu, triangular cage. But I get out of it, and ask directions of this father with the small girl. He can't help me either. It's as if people find their own *Metro* station by automatic pilot in a perpetually gridlocked and polluted city of over twenty million. And they complain about standing in rush hour trains at Slussen or Sankt Eriksplan in Stockholm...

Then I have found my station, with the help of a stern carpet shop proprietess, and am back in the system, avoiding the corridor walkways allocated to women and children only, which lead to platform spaces allocated to them alone. A man has either to retrace his steps or intrude illegally on a designated female carriage at certain times of day. I look at an inscrutable map I have been given somewhere, and see I have to change lines. Struggling out through a silent mass of standing men I see a staircase. Nothing in London compares with what happens now; certainly not the Paolozzi decorations at Tottenham Court Road. Because here is a corridor where the ceiling above is a planetarium – I take in the Milky Way. And after that, a series of panels shining in the footstep-echoing dark depicts the month-by-month development of the foetus in the womb.

In the *Tunnelbana* and the London Underground you know all the time where you are from the maps on the carriage walls. On the wall above the seats in my next Mexico City train to which I have changed an arcane line of small pale symbols (duck, fountain, lake, tree) denotes, I gather, the stations named in tiny print underneath them. This narrow carriage, like the last, is packed with people who push and elbow their way in and out silently, without courtesies.

There are courtesies in Bucharest. There is space for them in the wide trains, manufactured with foresight in the 1980s, that offer only hard plastic seats down the sides; there is hardly any sense of overcrowding. No one carries anything much in their hands between any two stations in Bucharest, between, say, Piața Victoriei and Iancului, Lidia Vianu's station; though Lidia, eminent Romanian scholar of modern British verse, might be carrying a bunch of small volumes by English poets. One day at Green Park it seems that in any train in London people increasingly carry more and more things around: small, black, obstructive backpacks, broad portfolios scanned on laps in rush hours, glossy carrier bags fixed upright between their feet. When did I last look at a bag and its owner wondering what it might contain?

A Bob Dylan tribute busker at Earls Court is shunned with embarrassed indifference. When we are stuck in the tunnel three or four stations along the District Line, the driver can see him through cameras not visible to us, a technology President Ceaușescu lacked and might have liked. Our surveillant driver says "We seem to have picked up a parasite. Please don't feed him." Through the tight press of the *Metro* crowd when it stops at Hidalgo, a girl enters the carriage, possibly as old at fifteen, in one hand a blaring, battery-powered CD player, in the other the CDs she sells. It could be that the CD I buy for ten pesos is blank; but it's wrapped up in cellophane with a picture of its Salsa band, and I don't think so. At Piaţa Unirii in Bucharest a gypsy boy of about seven joins my train and goes the spacious length of the carriage playing on a miniature squeeze-box. And goes on through an opening into the next carriage. And the next. Because you can see down the entire airy length of some Bucharest *Metro* trains while they are moving in a straight line. There is the boy, still playing and collecting in the distance; until the wide train turns a curve after Piaţa Romậna, and he vanishes.

In the vestibule at Baker Street, a quarrel. A boy tops up his Oyster card (store of so much of his identity) on a screen showing his recent journeys. His girl companion accuses him of having seen another girl in Fulham Broadway that afternoon. At Oceania (with its water symbol) I insert my hand between the bodies of several men in sombreros, find the hand of my own companion, and dare not let go of her in case she is left behind. I begin pulling when we are still two stations short of our destination; you have to start early from the middle of the carriage to get anywhere near the door in Mexico City. But where are so many men going, grimly stacked hundreds to a carriage at eight-thirty in the evening in Mexico City?

Home, said the taxi-driver. Next morning I am in his red-and-white vehicle (the safe sort; you are advised to avoid the green-and-white VW Beetle taxis). We are stuck at a traffic lights where a man passes among the halted traffic offering a book: *The Rules of Grammar For All Levels*. The men in the *Metro* last night had been "to the football", the driver tells me; and were miserable because their side had lost. London passengers would have behaved differently, far worse, I inform him. None of this Latin introversion, I think.

Another thing: it's a myth that the English go on queuing. I push out of a packed train into daylight at Piccadilly Circus to catch a bus going up Regent's Street, and see people clustering almost furtively a few yards away from the stop; then swooping and scrambling when the bus arrives. Whereas Mexicans are queuing, for buses and in shops, or to have some kind of ritual massage of head and shoulders, in the sunshine outside Zócalo station; where a man passes wearing a t-shirt declaring I WANT YOUR SKULL. It is getting dark on a sunny Saturday, and the Metropolitan Cathedral is closing.

Under its huge shadow a seething crowd fills the centre of the great square, and applauds speeches. A troop of wild performers from a far province dances and plays in the cause of Andres Manuel Lopez Obrádor, who has just formed a "cabinet in exile". At the end they throw cakes and apples to the enthusiastic crowd, who cheer. One of them sees a foreigner applauding, and pins a red, white and green flag on his lapel. Göran Persson, the Social Democrat prime minister soon to be rejected, without fraudulence, by the most finely-attuned political system in the world (in Sweden you can alter your postal vote by computer on the day if you change your mind after mailing it) is speaking outside Åhlens at the end of the election campaign.

I check with a party worker that it was not Åhlens, but another department store, where Anna Lindh, Swedish foreign minister, was stabbed and killed by a madman in broad daylight four years ago. Down this long narrow pedestrianised street, in the middle of the prime minister's peroration, marches the noisy, pompous royal band. It's on its way to the Old Town, an ancient Saturday tradition; and the boss has to stop for it. During the pause, a representative of the Christian Democrats gives me a toffee wrapped in the logo of their party. I eat this toffee ten weeks later when it comes out of my pocket with the last Mexico metro ticket, and with the Romanian leaflet offering a cure for psoriasis, taken automatically as I came up from the tunnel and blinked outside Universitate station. In the daylight outside Oxford Circus this afternoon an evangelical preacher bellows through a megaphone, and a girl presses me to take a card offering 'phone deals for anywhere other than places I often want to call: Bucharest, Stockholm, Mexico City, London. I suppose I am home.

Alan Brownjohn's latest volume is *Collected Poems* (Enitharmon, 2006).

Under the Influence: new series

The Poetry Society's *Under the Influence* series has proved a popular and critical success in exploring how today's poets engage with, learn from, explore and acknowledge poets of the past. This year's series invites leading names in our current poetry world to expand on the influence of significant twentieth-century figures in shaping their own endeavours and poetic sensibilities.

10 May 2007: Jo Shapcott on Marianne Moore
21 June 2007: Maurice Riordan on Seamus Heaney
18 October 2007: Carol Rumens on Sylvia Plath
29 November 2007: Gwyneth Lewis on Stevie Smith

All events are chaired by **Anne-Marie Fyfe**
The London Review Bookshop, 14 Bury Place, London, WC1A 2JL. Nearest tube: Holborn

Tickets: £10 (£5 Poetry Society members, LRB subscribers and concs)
Season Ticket for all four events: £35 (£18 Poetry Society members, LRB subscribers and concs)
Box office: 020 7420 9895

THE POETRY SOCIETY

REVIEWS
&
PRIZES

Concentration, not of language, but of nerve.
—*David Morley*

A Paul Muldoon Roundtable

Horse Latitudes, Faber, £14.99, ISBN 9780571232345;
General Admission, Gallery, £10.95, ISBN 1852354100;
The End of the Poem, Faber, £25, ISBN 0571227406

Muldoon As Critic

SEAN O'BRIEN

P aul Muldoon the poet expects his readers to be on their toes; Paul Muldoon the critic has the same expectations but also provides a courteous, almost conversational presence, both in his first critical book, *To Ireland, I* (OUP, 2000) and the new collection of Oxford Lectures on Poetry, *The End of the Poem*. The courtesy extends to his practice as a reader and a critic: the effect of his enquiries into Yeats, Frost, Bishop, Emily Dickinson, Lowell, Montale and others is to make the reader feel that the subject has been intriguingly broached, not (as with quite a lot of criticism) that the matter has been exhausted (albeit honourably) without conspicuous benefit to pleasure or understanding. Yet it is never wholly clear where we have got to: a poem is encouraged to ramify in suggestiveness until Muldoon has filled his hour-long lecture with all manner of striking sidelights and possibilities. Then he takes his leave. An unsympathetic reader would claim that Muldoon rambles, but in Muldoon's book a ramble is a good way to take in the landscape. His title – *The End of the Poem* – is a pun, since in Muldoon's book poems probably don't have ends, but instead offer ways back into themselves, so off we go again, inexhaustibly.

Although Muldoon ranges widely, his method is consistent: etymology, echoes and the anagrammatical properties of words are what first fascinate him. More than once he repeats: *nomen est omen*. Muldoon's language-world has not been disenchanted, and partly as a result he can display both rigour (in his discussion of versions of Montale's 'L'Anguilla', for example) and a readiness to snap up a trifle that others might not think worth considering: if it can be found, it's there, which can make Muldoon's imaginative literalism a bit eerie.

It is also interesting that Muldoon's critical approach assumes a natural right to the best of both worlds – intensive close reading alongside biographical interest. Indeed, he seems at times disinclined to accept that there is a border which defines the poem as a particular thing rather than an example of everything else. Things *enter* the poem. Thus the lecture on 'The Literary Life', from Ted Hughes's posthumous collection *Birthday Letters*, involves a detailed consideration of the poem's real-world source in Marianne Moore's apparent dismissal of a batch of poems sent to her by Sylvia Plath and in Moore's unsuccessful attempt to rectify matters when encountering Hughes at a party after Plath's death. Hughes writes: "I listened, heavy as a graveyard, / While she searched for the grave / Where she could lay down her little wreath", and Muldoon concludes: "'The Literary Life' is not only an extraordinarily unabashed account of a particularly strong attack of the anxiety of influence, but it's impossible to read without a sense of the biographies of the main characters, without a regard for information available only beyond the bailiwick of the poem, including […] information about times, dates and places."

You might argue that this is to spare the poem the task of standing on its own two feet. Indeed, what Muldoon has in a sense done is to considerably increase the poem's interest by his own critical / biographical labours. There is, though, very unusually, a word in this poem that doesn't quite yield itself to Muldoon's attention. Moore's face is described as a "tiny American treen bobbin / On a spindle", and Muldoon glosses 'treen' as an archaic word meaning 'made of tree', there to indicate what is wooden and archaic in Moore's attitudes. To an English reader of Muldoon's generation, though, 'treen' also refers to the Treens. These were the army of pitiless skull-faced robots commanded by the Mekon, a dwarfish creature with a massive head, who bestrode the cosmos from a saucer-vehicle, and dominated the adventures of Dan Dare in the Eagle. Can this be admitted to the poem? The poem as Muldoon presents it is borderless, and the implication that there is something absurd, shrunken and imperiously monstrous about Moore seems to square with his interpretation, though it would of course be extremely unkind and – for all we know – inaccurate.

It is uncertain whether Muldoon will go on to decide whether there are, or should be, limits to interpretation. Writing about Lowell, an intensively autobiographical poet who seems to expect you to know the real life characters passing through his poems, Muldoon refers to the need for a poem to be "*relatively* free-standing", which keeps the options open. After all, he has made a writing life out of seeing what might be possible. Why should he set frontiers to his enquiries? One thing is sure: Muldoon's gifts extend to criticism as well as poetry. His essays strike the difficult balance between due complexity and readability. Even people who normally give literary criticism a wide berth could find a good deal of stimulus and pleasure in *The End of the Poem*. Let's hope some of them give it a try.

Sean O'Brien's 'Blue Night' and 'The Them' appear on pp. 5–6.

❧

Horse Latitudes

PETER MCDONALD

Is poetry a game? Or, more relevantly perhaps, what kind of a game is Paul Muldoon's poetry? Does it, for example, have rules? In 'It Is What It Is', the poet seems to be propelled (for no immediately apparent reason) from the unwrapping of a present for his young son in contemporary America to a sitting-room in 1950s Co. Antrim, and:

> the inlaid cigarette-box, the shamrock-painted jug,
> the New Testament bound in red leather
> lying open, Lordie, on her lap
> while I mull over the rules of this imperspicuous game
> that seems to be missing one piece, if not more.

Already, with the poem only half over, there are puzzles here, some of them easier to solve than others. "Imperspicuous" is one: "not perspicuous or clear; obscure" says the *OED*, warning that the word is *rare*, and giving a sole instance (from 1721). "Lordie" is another: this time, the puzzle is not so much semantic as tonal, for this interjected exclamation smacks of kitsch, as though Muldoon's voice was suddenly experiencing some kind of interference from Al Jolson, or an old American sitcom. As the poem concludes, Muldoon proffers more pieces of the puzzle:

> My mother. Shipping out for good. For good this time.
> The game. The plaything spread on the rug.
> The fifty years I've spent trying to put it together.

The poem is tight, in a certain formal sense, with carefully interlaced rhymes; but it is loose syntactically, as the failure of these last lines to produce real sentences indicates. Is, for example, "The game" the same thing as "The plaything spread on the rug"? What, in that case, is the "it" of the last line? And what would those "fifty years" be doing if they were indeed to find themselves as the subjects in a sentence? We don't know; does Muldoon?

One response might be simple: Muldoon doesn't know these things, and that's precisely the point of the poem. However, both *Horse Latitudes* and its companion-volume of Oxford lectures, *The End of the Poem*, reveal a writer who is keen – very keen – to suggest that poetry is full of puzzles which, with the right equipment, are capable of solution. Muldoon invests very heavily in what might be called an hermetic theory of reading – which is also, as he acknowledges, a theory of writing. The finding of clues, and the apparently wayward, the counter-intuitive or sometimes plain irrational methods of piecing these together, lead Muldoon deep into intertextual mazes in, and between, his chosen poems and poets. To look for an argument in *The End of the Poem* would be to look for the wrong thing, for Muldoon is engaged rather on a complicated series of displays, both of his learning and of himself as a reader and writer. Repeatedly, Muldoon explores a poem to show that everything connects (in ways always more or less arcane) with everything else, and that nothing is too odd, or too unlikely, to be good material for such connections. It all adds up, Muldoon suggests; but he refrains from saying what it all adds up to.

Horse Latitudes seems to live by the same rules as its critical companion and, because Muldoon has been for so long so very eye-catching a poet, one whose style of writing has been both intoxicating and infectious, it's possible to go with the flow of these poems, enjoying them for their Muldoon-like qualities without pausing to wonder too much about the particular games that are being played. And perhaps settling for the "imperspicuous" here is enough. Certainly, there are poems that can stand alone as powerful – I would instance 'Turkey Buzzards' above all, along with 'Tithonus', 'Eggs' and 'The Landing'. But even an enthusiastic reader of Muldoon must be pulled up short by some of the material, where the very scale of the intellectual machinery, and its great, hermetically labouring noise, are close to overwhelming. There are some errors in scale – 'The Old Country' is far too long, for example, as are the '90 Instant Messages to Tom Moore'. In both cases, the problem is one that has bedevilled Muldoon for a long time: an excess of formalism meeting an excess of clue-dropping. The 'Horse Latitudes' sequence itself strains under the burden of wanting to say something about the woeful politics of the world and not finding a direct language adequate to its purposes. 'Sillyhow Stride', in which Muldoon mixes private grief (for his sister) with celebrity grief (for Warren Zevon) seems to me (though I would admit to not being necessarily perspicacious) an empty performance, one shot down completely by the over-generous injections of lines written by John Donne. Insofar as the poetry communicates (and this is so for the book as a whole), it conveys an awareness of death: there is certainly a chill to be felt, but Muldoon seems to have little to tell us about that which we don't know already. Perhaps, as with much successful contemporary poetry, it is precisely the banality of the meaning which appeals, and which enables the obscurity, the endlessly-proliferating formal self-involvement, and the unconstrained instability of the diction to pass muster. At this stage in his career (though not, I think, at some earlier stages), a Muldoon poem has little new to say: instead, and with a certain bristling defensiveness, it is what it is. By Muldoon's own best standards, this isn't really enough.

Peter McDonald's latest collection is *The House of Clay* (Carcanet, 2007).

ℬ

Muldoon's New Poems And Lyrics

STEVEN MATTHEWS

To start in with the titles: *Horse Latitudes*, Paul Muldoon's eleventh collection from Faber, is glossed in the book's blurb as the navigational zone north and south of the equator "in which stasis if not stagnation is the order of the day"; the area where sailors once threw horses into the ocean to conserve supplies. By contrast, *General Admission* denotes Muldoon's gathering of lyrics written for his equivocally-named rock band 'Rackett' (the rear-jacket photo of whom unequivocally brings to mind Muldoon's own earlier poem – hey – 'Paunch'). 'General Admission' is interestingly slippery, its seemingly genial acceptingness carrying resonant charge from a confessional 'admission of' something, as well as Shakespearean possibility in 'the general', the public, who are somehow being allowed to engage with these lyrics. The two titles knock against each other. On the one hand, the more contained, but self-proclaimedly in-the-doldrums, collection from the main poetry publisher, swathed in its George Stubbs cover picture. On the other, the cartoonic Gallery cover suggesting that the besuited poet can really (for good or ill, and without condescension) let it hang loose.

The rock lyrics let in 'the general' in a surprising way also; often being voiced by stereotypical low- or no-lifes, intriguingly cast as urbane corporate-climbers, social creepers and PhD students on the make (in every sense). Street names, the names of pavement cafés, of beauty products and gizmos, leap off every page, and jostle wittily alongside relics of high culture and history:

> To think you used to scold [...]
> My saying Paris Hilton
> And Haile Selassie
> And Carrière's *Milton*
> And your own sweet chassis
> Were cast in the same mold

The typical zest with which the syntax of this stanza skips around the alarming rhymes towards its inevitable destination (Selassie/chassis) reminds us, as if we needed it, that, for all of his supposedly appealing 'post-modern' openness, Muldoon's master remains, as always (and for ill *and* good), the old *seigneur* Byron. The question, then, becomes one as to how far we should indulge the indulgence of this mid-career Muldoon, replete with the old vim, but seemingly unable to find something different to say (if able self-consciously to advertise the fact)? Like later Byron, the worry is that he has become glutted on the success of his own knack ("You think I'm Mr Right," as one opening lyric line has it), and that he's now gone 'Wrong'. Form remains while the content, the ability to carry the poetic quest forward, has possibly leached away. The 'general admission' is one of knowing cosiness, sounding off to no end.

Such knowledge also weighs upon Muldoon's new collection of poetry, signal again in its deployment of formal ambition, but troublingly inert in terms of its content. As the third part of this recent outpouring, *The End of the Poem*, seems to suggest – for all the lectures' glancing across etymologies and aural consonances of poetry in search of a key to unlock it – poets are inveterate self-rewriters. They carry with them a stock of imagery, modes, and possible formal choices from work to work, which then amount to their signature. The becalmed *Horse Latitudes* wears and performs this knowledge as one of its surface traits. Muldoon's 1998 *Hay* had seen him buoyantly 'mid-career', seemingly waiting for "something to take flight". Yet, as Clair Wills was the first to point out about *Hay*, both the opening sequence and its closing sonnets redeployed the same ninety rhyme sounds from 'Incantata' (Muldoon's great, sonorous elegy for the artist Mary Farl Powers) and

'Yarrow' (partly about the death of his mother) from his previous collection. Those same ninety rhymes have since appeared in the final sequence of the intermediary collection between *Hay* and *Horse Latitudes*, 'At the Sign of the Black Horse, September 1999' from *Moy Sand and Gravel*. They now recur *once again* in the final elegy from the new collection, 'Sillyhow Stride', for the record producer Warren Zevon. Rarely if ever in the history of poetry has this complex formal self-restraint and repetition been played out across such expanses of poetry. The doldrums indicated by the title of the new collection are a sign of repeatedly played out ending, of death writ o'er all.

Horse Latitudes 'book ends' *Hay* in other formal senses: through its sequence of ninety rhymed haikus, its sonnet sequence (here a rather obvious juxtaposition of battles ancient and modern with a love affair) and other 'exploded' sonnet forms. In genre terms here again is a riddle (its answer a disappointing 'griddle'), and a re-skewing of the joyously skewed everyday sayings or *saws* from the earlier collection's 'Symposium' ("To have your cake is to pay Paul"). Now, in 'The Old Country', we have, significantly, thirteen sonnets on the same idea (Muldoon is as much a numerologist as Yeats or Dante). This is an old country where nothing changes, since "Every track was an inside track / and every job an inside job."

Where *Hay* had derived much poetic possibility from its delight in the 'what ifs' of life, and *Moy Sand and Gravel* from the exploration of ancestral pasts, both those familiar, and those with which Muldoon ("the goy from the Moy") had become entwined through marriage, it is difficult to discover what the stringencies of *Horse Latitudes* cohere around, beyond what have now become signature 'Muldoon' themes. Another sonnet here, 'Glaucus', reprises 'Yarrow' in its knowledge that the preservation of the purest possibility, "out of the fray", can lead the artist to self-destruction. Glaucus is "eaten now by his own mares", formerly kept from common "horse toils."

While the reminder that the quotidian securities and order of individual worlds are vulnerable to threatening forces from beyond, and finally to death, is *personally* unbearable, to be repeatedly reminded of it *poetically* is to become aware that something more needs to be said. Repeated aural return to this primal scene, at whatever extension and with whatever numerological inventiveness, overwhelms and stalls the poetic career. The druggy zaniness of 'Sillyhow Stride' is a weak resonance of life-asserting residues in 'Incantata', and in turn threatens to subsume the more truly realised feeling in the elegy, embedded within this to Zevon, for Muldoon's sister. Unless Muldoon finds a way beyond current stasis, his poetry will become increasingly bloated by more of the same, and more of the same again.

Steven Matthews's latest book is *Modernism*, in the Arnold Context Series.

The Sudden World

ALAN BROWNJOHN

Louis MacNeice, *Collected Poems* edited by Peter McDonald,
Faber, £30, ISBN 9780571215744

This welcome centenary edition of everything a great modern poet published (plus a selection from a large number of poems that he didn't) is a huge enterprise to cover in a rapid summary. Readers should unquestionably fork out £30 for an absorbing 836 pages; but where should a reviewer begin with his own complimentary copy?

Perhaps at a revealing moment of the poet's self-awareness near the beginning. In a 'Foreword' to his first book, published in 1929, while he was still an Oxford undergraduate, Louis McNeice wrote, "I have called the collection *Blind Fireworks* because they are artificial and yet random; because they go quickly through their antics against an important background, and fall, and go out quickly." Youthful mock-modesty, but there was truth in it, an awareness of the risks involved in being good at the pyrotechnics; and besides, well-organised, venturesome and prolific already. And yet *Blind Fireworks* itself is appropriately included in this *Collected* as an appendix rather than a prelude, because it is really no more than a work of erratic promise, groping among what became MacNeice's characteristic mix of themes: love, landscape, art, myth, time – and memory: "But sometimes on my mind's flat morphiac pond / Memories like swans would float, and dip / Their necks like teaspoons plumbing my beyond."

All the same, by 1935, the year *Poems* appeared, MacNeice had written poems that still rise, spark and explode today, obstinately refusing to "go out". Among his best-known pieces there are 'The Creditor' (from 1929, only just missing *Blind Fireworks*): "The quietude of a soft wind / Will not rescind / My debts to God, but gentle-skinned / His finger probes". And 'Snow': "World is suddener than we fancy it / World is crazier and more of it than we think". If that original puzzling idea of "an important background" hinted vaguely at a fear that his kind of poetry might come to seem too gay an activity at an alarming moment in history, he has by now begun to deliver an emphatic message that time is short given the way the world is going.

The Earth Compels (1938) contains well-known items such as 'Carrickfergus', with its hints of a future war in its dark recall of a past one; 'The Sunlight on the Garden' ("soon, my friend / We shall have no time for dances") and the hilarious and ominous 'Bagpipe Music', still irresistibly quotable on the atmosphere of the late 1930s:

> It's no go my honey love, it's no go my poppet;
> Work your hands from day to day, the winds will blow the profit.
> The glass is falling hour by hour, the glass will fall for ever,
> But if you break the bloody glass you won't hold up the weather.

From this, the penultimate poem in this third volume of mainly short ones, MacNeice graduated to the length of *Autumn Journal*, which occupies sixty-three pages in this book.

Conceived, he says in a prefatory 'Note', as "something half-way between the lyric and the didactic poem", it offers an enthralling day-by-day inter-weaving of private and public events (love, teaching, politics, international tension) through the days of the Munich negotiations – "posters flapping on the railings tell the fluttered / World that Hitler speaks" – and the uneasy months that followed them:

> These days are misty, insulated, mute [...]
> People have not recovered from the crisis,
> Their faces are far away, the tone of the words
> Belies their thesis.
> For they say that now it is time unequivocally to act,
> To let the pawns be taken [...]

With its narrative verve and pace, its directness and honesty, above all its accuracy and clarity about the experience of daily life, *Autumn Journal* is really the only successful long poem MacNeice ever achieved, one of a very few poems of that length in that period; just to list Auden's *New Year Letter, For the Time Being, The Sea and the Mirror* and *The Age of Anxiety* is to recite a roll-call of misfortunes.

The next three volumes of MacNeice shorter poems are *Plant and Phantom* (1941), *Springboard* (1944) and *Holes in the Sky* (1948.) In the first two, familiar titles and openings flash up regularly as a reminder that he could be a poet of timelessly topical lyrics: take 'Prognosis' ("Goodbye, Winter / The days are getting longer, / The tea-leaf in the teacup / Is herald of a stranger"); or 'Meeting Point' ("Time was away and somewhere else"); or 'The Satirist' ("Who is that man with the handshake? Don't you know [...]"). But by the end of *Holes in the Sky* he is into the morass of 'The Stygian Banks':

> if we stopped haggling, stopped as we did in the raids,
> The gap in our personal racket, as in the gunfire,
> Should become positive, crystal; which is the end of the news,
> Which is the beginning of wisdom. No captions and no jargon,
> No diminution, distortion or sterilisation of entity [...]

Which could be true; yet one waits in vain for the rocket to rise.

This proved a prelude to the techniques of *Ten Burnt Offerings* (1952) and *Autumn Sequel* (1954) – which takes up 119 pages in this *Collected*, twice the length of the *Journal* with much less to say. What has happened? The fireworks have gone, the ruminative, rhetorical MacNeice (the latter word his own choice) has emerged to take over, in quest of an achievement to bolster his reputation in the middle of his career. In the first of those two books he pursued "a dialectical structure", in the second he aimed at a pattern of "digressions which aren't really digressions" (quoted by Jon Stallworthy in his excellent, definitive biography of the poet). No wonder inspiration flags, except in places where an earlier lyric fluency or a genuine emotional pressure returns – as in 'The Death of a Cat' in the 1952 volume.

Both books seem to renounce the mood and achievement of the earlier work. So it was surprising – fast forward – to sceptical younger critics that the final three volumes, *Visitations* (1957), *Solstices* (1961) and *The Burning Perch* (1963, published just ten days after he died) saw a convincing return to form. In the title-poem of *Visitations* he declares that the Muse might arrive for poets in any momentous form – the cradle, the clock, the coffin – to "burst the cordon / Which isolates them from their inmost vision". It was gratifying, then, for loyal admirers who almost idolised MacNeice as the social observer of the 1930s and the creative impresario of BBC radio Home Service and Third Programme in the 1940s and 1950s, that in his last poems the Muse was again there in things like pub games, breakfasts in foreign hotels, landscapes seen through night train windows, rooms transformed in mirrors, pillar boxes, taxis and soap suds. The world stayed "suddener" for Louis MacNeice at the end.

Alan Brownjohn's latest volume is *Collected Poems* (Enitharmon, 2006).

Herma, Herminche, Hermione-ohne-o!

DAVID MORLEY

John Fuller, *The Space of Joy*, Chatto and Windus, £10.99, ISBN 0701181109;
Brendan Kennelly, *Now*, Bloodaxe, £8.95, ISBN 1852247495

What happens when the tectonic plates of poetry and prose fiction wedge together? Do they fracture, meld, throw up mountains? The practice of the novelist and poet John Fuller offers illuminating answers (mountains among them). Of course, some novelists regard poetry as a kind of super-calculus to their own prosaic long divisions of character and scene making. Poems train the inner ear; and help you write without verbal padding. Such prosers slink through the lit cages of form, metrics and patterns to hone style, to invite poetic form to offer new ways of saying. Many choose the short story as a place for such trials, for testing narrative nerve over a tight distance, and for organising a palette. Later, these lessons find release across a novel's vasty fields. Yet why not make such gestures through poems? With John Fuller, you get everything at once: a show of the possibilities of long forms for which verse has the final word – if form can be seen as an element of language (although I imagine Fuller never forgets that form itself *is* fiction).

In previous books – and as superbly in *The Space of Joy* – Fuller uses the book-length poetic sequence as a means for creating inter-penetrating narratives. Within the sequence, he tests and subverts smaller poetic forms against their ability and his own skill to harness and carry numerous stories and scenes with economy – and release the surprises that spring from tight pattern. The total effect is vivid and challenging. What Fuller also does here – as he did in *The Illusionists* (1980), his verse novel about art dealing – is create a kind of prismatic narrative-poem that splits and splices multiple scenes, dialogue and stories.

The practice has much in common with the interlinking narratives of the film-makers Krzysztof Kieslowski and Alejandro González Iñárritu; and *The Space of Joy* lends itself to that kind of adaptation. Visual details are emotionally, adventurously specific – "a train is puffing into the station / Like an old gentleman expecting treats" – and the sound effects are those of a sensitive listener to the origins of words as well as to the natural world –

"the troglodytic-troglodytic wren / Twitching her stuck tail like a rabbit's scut". John Fuller records his long poems with every one of his senses, but he always edits and scores them with his entire mind.

That is some part of his technique. What is the story? *The Space of Joy* revolves around the failures and compromises of love and art – of life and art to be Mahlerian about it – probing the lives of Petrarch, Coleridge, Matthew Arnold, Brahms and Wallace Stevens. Fuller allows the poem to explore the emotional lives of these artists through sympathetic biography, but also by slipping on the attitudes of the artists through ventriloquistic writing. The section on Wallace Stevens opens a curtain on the author's voice – on when that voice has aged into the hazard of mere mannerism:

> I am the amateur of tragedy.
> The Knave of Hearts, the Quince of Ives,
> My fingers laddering the ivories,
> Idly chromatic, quintessence of black and white,
> White of the inner thigh, the black of lace
> And all that jazz, the hootchie-cootchie-coo.

You do not have to be interested in the lives of these artists to get a great deal from these readings of their joys and despairs. You do however need a taste for character, and an instinct that character is always story, and even destiny; as well as for how the apparently greatest among us can be seen as ultimately ridiculous in the wrong – or worse still, the right – light. In Fuller's world, landscape – an apparently balmy Swiss landscape here – can also be character. His carefully observed and vivid natural landscape carries its own precise connotations, edges for wildness and the unpredictable.

This is not some new versifying of literary nonfictional biography; Fuller is too gifted and inventive a creator of character to tell the whole truth and nothing but. As Jean Cocteau once urged (and who else would), "Cultivate your flaws. They are the truest thing about you". In Fuller's world, Coleridge natters and wrestles with his Shadow Folk and himself; Brahms puffs fat cigars and clumsily composes ("Herma, Herminche, Hermione-ohne-o!"); while Arnold can't help himself noticing breasts, "Commas nestled together / Sweet in their cotton mosaic". Brahms declared elsewhere, "It is not hard to compose, but it is wonderfully hard to let the superfluous notes fall under the table". Sometimes the things we leave out, and the shortfalls of our character, are essential to our character. They might even be our character because they under the table. One of the things John Fuller understands is that fiction writers are not really storytellers in method. They are story-makers and -shapers, as poets are makers and shapers of verse. The final value of fiction rests in that making and rewriting – those unneeded notes falling beneath the table. Made well and shaped well, fiction becomes believable – more life than lie – and far less innocuous. Fuller does this all so well in verse that one is left believing that the poetic sequence might yield more potential than a novella, allowing greater character and theme development than a short story, without the intricate structural exigencies or the Niagaran tight-rope walk of a novel.

In fact, Fuller's experiments offer the concentration of a short story and the wider compass of the novel's form. He really pushes against the received wisdom of how much poetry can contain. Yet the term 'experimental' is barely breathed in connection with Fuller: catalogued as he is as a post-Movement poet, academic and technician in a time when those three terms are thought to be treasons to emotion and community, or enemies of usefulness. Fuller's work is far better, braver, and weirder than it is made out to be. And Fuller's type of weird seems a great tradition – his skill sets so high a mark that it appears at once radical and strange to those accustomed to being offered somewhat less.

One of the lessons offered by Fuller's portrayal of arty protagonists is that we become what we seem to be: hardly a comforting thought in this present age of 'finding oneself'. Brendan Kennelly's *Now* exerts itself in a preoccupation with present identity, but instead of making a story from the conflict of being and seeming, Kennelly opts for an aphoristic sound-bite poetry which sometimes hits, sometimes misses. I am sure he does not mind either way, for missing the mark in life and art is no small part of the point of this book. It is an interesting adventure as a sequence, a kind of nano-poetry (his tercets seem almost centrifuged in philosophic concentration).

However, despite their brevity, part of their energy arises from a concentration not of language but of nerve. As Don Paterson has written with his typical scotch-and-soda of dare and lucidity, "The shorter the form, the greater our expectation of its significance – and the greater its capacity for disappointing us". With regard to Kennelly's book, less is perhaps not always more. *Now* makes for immediacy (although who cares for *now* in our so-immediate world); I would argue the book feels like a displacement activity for the poet's longer-haul tasks, shaped so interestingly across his controversial book-length sequences *Cromwell* (1983) and *The Book of Judas* (1991). There is a fracture here between endeavour and form, and Kennelly's enterprise suffers in comparison to Fuller's ease with scale and narrative progression/subversion. Read both, but in separate rooms, on different days.

David Morley's next collection of poetry is *The Invisible Kings* (Carcanet, 2007).

Achieving Independence

STEPHEN KNIGHT

Jacob Polley, *Little Gods*, Picador, £8.99, ISBN 9780330444200;
Jean 'Binta' Breeze, *The Fifth Figure*, Bloodaxe, £8.95, ISBN 9781852247324

The final word of Jacob Polley's *Little Gods* is "darkness", and variations of that word recur throughout this second volume, along with owls, honey, smoke, mirrors and sleep. The source of the book's sombreness is not made clear. Absence and the weather prevail – Polley is a fine observer of rain, wind and snow – and a low-key surrealism yields pleasingly odd images; one speaker likens his head to a beehive into which someone puffs smoke before reaching inside. The writing is poised, mysteriously fearful to the point of torpor, deceptively plain and, at times, almost child-like in its directness:

> The sun rises, the sun falls.
> Rats run up and down the walls.
> Mushrooms grow in amber rings.
> Graveyards spread their marble wings.

All in all, a crafted book of poems. And yet... After the above quote had sent me to James Fenton's 'The Killer Snails', I began to hear echoes of Simon Armitage, Paul Farley, Robert Crawford and Craig Raine, while the use of motifs recalled Paul Muldoon, and the final poem's appearance after a few blank pages reminded me of Don Paterson's *God's Gift to Women*. None of these impressions dominate the volume, but they make it seem very familiar; I was struck by how comfortably its poetry would sit alongside, for example, the early verse of the Poet Laureate, a man almost a quarter of a century older than Polley. It is perhaps unfair to see this well-written book as symptomatic of the doldrums in British poetry, but it would be more exciting to read a youngish poet (Jacob Polley is thirty-one) who challenges fashion rather than falls into line with it. Philip Larkin was, after all, only eight years younger than Dylan Thomas, who was seven years younger than Auden – three very dissimilar poets.

A family memoir tracing Jean 'Binta' Breeze's mixed ancestry from the nineteenth-century to the present, *The Fifth Figure* is an appropriate hybrid of prose and poetry, the latter topping and tailing the volume. The book consists of a single 13-line lyric and five monologues of "women who begat / Like in Genesis". Beginning with Emmeline, an orphan who arrives in Jamaica to live with her missionary brother, it closes with the poet herself, whose "poems and songs of Jamaica / Had taken me all round the world". Motifs include the quadrille, unwanted pregnancies and abusive men, though the drama of the work's many intriguing episodes is never fully explored, because *The Fifth Figure* frustratingly races through the years. It would have benefited from being a good deal longer. The prose is one-paced and prone to cliche, events pile up, and there is little time to linger. Given Jean 'Binta' Breeze's pedigree as actress, film writer and theatre director, the stiltedness of her dramatic writing is a surprise. Only 'Figure Four' and the title poem (the poet's own monologue) achieve independence; one is a *tour de force,* spoken in a child's voice which develops with the narrative, the other is the only section completely in verse. 'Figure Three', for example, opens with a piece of clumsy shorthand: "It was in this village that I, Amanda Magdalene Wood, grew up."

The Fifth Figure is, for all this, a refreshingly unfamiliar, fascinating act of retrieval. Perhaps Jean 'Binta' Breeze will continue to mine her material in future work.

Stephen Knight's *Sardines and Other Poems* (Young Picador) was published in 2004.

☙

American Beauty

SARAH CROWN

Frederick Seidel, *Selected Poems,* Faber, £14.99, ISBN 0571226396;
Marilyn Hacker, *Essays on Departure,* Carcanet, £12.95, ISBN 1903039789;
Jane Hirshfield, *After,* Bloodaxe, £8.95, ISBN 185224741

"Frederick Seidel" declared Calvin Bedient in a 2001 article for the *Boston Review*, "is the poet the century deserved". If claiming the entire century for him smacks of hyperbole, his role as a scathing arbiter of the twentieth-century American experience is beyond dispute. The first poem in Faber's generous *Selected* opens onto a quintessentially American vista: "A football spirals through the oyster glow / Of dawn dope and fog in LA's / Bel Air, punted perfectly." The image of the football soaring through the radiant sky is one of pure hope, the languorous "spirals" suggestive of cinematic slow-motion. It is as if, in an echo of Stanley Kubrick's club-into-satellite sequence at the beginning of *2001: A Space Odyssey*, Seidel is spinning his country into existence on the page. But this moment of perfection is transitory; the "spiral" rapidly becomes downward. Poem and collection fall away from the opening image into a world of death and drugs, grubby politics and empty fame.

Like Hemingway and Fitzgerald before him, Seidel's clear-eyed contempt for his country's excesses gains heft and bite from his participation in them. His poems brim with glossy symbols of decadence – expensive cocktails, beautiful women, a red Ducati 916 – but he is acutely aware of the blankness behind the glamour: a woman who "watches the sunrise in her martini" is seen just lines later with "tubes in her nostrils and arms." Sunrise, in fact, is a powerful motif for Seidel throughout the volume's two-and-a-half decades, its appeal deriving, perhaps, from the way its significance shifts as the day passes: unblemished promise in the morning; unrealised potential by afternoon. In one description of the daybreak in which his flair for richly yielding imagery is exhibited, he encapsulates this duality:

> White-faced gold bulging the horizon
> Like too much honey in a spoon […]

Although the "gold" and "honey" set the lines aglow, there is "too much": spillage is inevitable. Once again, conspicuous consumption produces instant gratification but stores up trouble for the future. Seidel's poems are hymns to corrupted innocence, glittering, merciless mirrors held up to 20th-century America's surfeit.

In Marilyn Hacker's *Essays on Departure*, we have the selected poems of another great American poet, but there the similarity between these books ends. Where Seidel is mordant and aloof, Hacker is frank, sensuous, luxuriantly experiential; where his lines meander insouciantly, she revels in the productive discipline of tight form. She makes great play with enjambment, as in the lengthy 'Graffiti from the Gare Saint-Manque', in which she describes the experience of being "another Jewish lesbian in France". "The sheet was too soft," she says, of the bed she shares with her lover, "Unwashed for three weeks, / it smelled like both of us. The sin we are / beset by is despair." The sense of the stanza pivots on the break of the second line; what seems at first to be a reference to the "sin" of their relationship ("the sin we are") is turned on its head – "despair", not love, is the sin here.

Such deft enjambment has the effect not only of sending meaning rippling back and forth along the lines, but of braiding those lines more closely into the poems. On occasion, as in the sonnet sequence 'Eight Days in April' (a pressingly vivid account of the lust, tumult, violence and ecstasy of the first days of a love affair), this braiding moves beyond the individual poems. Each sonnet begins by recycling the final line of its predecessor, while the first line of the first sonnet ("I broke a glass, got bloodstains on the sheet") is also the last line of the last. The interwoven structure enacts both the intense connection and the desirable isolation that come with new passion. The sequence and its protagonists look inwards, safely sealed off from the outside world. As the years pass and her poems pile up with losses – deaths, goodbyes, the sacrifice of her breast to "a grasping tumor" – the focus of Hacker's passion shifts from the sexual. Her latest work, written after her treatment for cancer, pulses instead with undifferentiated ardour for what she calls the "gifts of the quotidian". The joy with which she praises the "light which frames a building that I see / daily, walking home from the bakery" and the "sudden green / and scarlet window-box geraniums / backlit in cloud-encouraged clarity" is palpable. Her lines, saturated with light and dazzling colour, revivify the world for her readers as it has been revivified for her.

Sensuousness – or more specifically a sensory appreciation of the natural world – is the defining feature of the latest collection from the pen of the last of our American trio, Jane Hirshfield. Where nature in Marilyn Hacker's work is broadly reflexive, a weathervane for her state of mind, Hirshfield is drawn rather to its innocence, its freedom from emotion and reflection. After the density of Seidel and Hacker, her spare, uncluttered poetry cleanses the palate like a sorbet; her desire to leave the natural world to itself, free from the weight of pathetic fallacy, produces an invigorating minimalism. "Sky" she claims briskly, and with something approaching relief,

> offers no model, no mirror – cloudy or bright –
> to the ordinary heart: which is secretive,
> rackety, domestic […]

The division that she establishes in her poetry between the self and the world finds its echo in a Lacanian perception of an irredeemably fragmented self, the investigation of which drives the collection. "I wanted to be intimate to my own life", she sighs, embarking on a ceaseless quest for wholeness, the inevitable failure of which expresses itself as an envy of animals who, lacking an awareness of 'I', have access to a singularity of experience that is denied her: a dog with a bone is "fallen into the marrow-pleasure completely"; when a cat "waits in the hedge-path / No cell of her body is not waiting." The simple elegance of her lines is deceptive; this is a profound, insightful collection.

Sarah Crown is the editor of *Guardian Unlimited Books*.

℘

A Pioneering Dialect

CHARLOTTE NEWMAN

Robert Gray, *Nameless Earth*, Carcanet, £9.95, ISBN 9781857548389;
Les Murray, *The Biplane Houses*, Carcanet, £8.95, ISBN 9781857548938;
Peter Porter, *Eighteen Poems*, £5, Shoestring Press, ISBN 1904886426;
John Tranter, *Urban Myths: 210 Poems*, £15.99, Salt, ISBN 9781844712526

In 'A Jackeroo in Kensington', John Tranter quotes Peter Porter: "The eyes that look into Australia / are European eyes […]". The eyes of all four of these poets, looking out from Australia, are very much Australian; they look into Europe frequently, as into the rest of the world; but they are thoroughly rooted in the Antipodean tradition, and committed to further establishing that tradition. It is even possible to detect a note of anti-imperialist bitterness towards old world literary history in Tranter's work:

> With a fistful of dollars in a knapsack
> and a brutal turn of phrase, colonials
> are crashing the party. *Cette parade sauvage* –
> on the skyline you can see Rupert Murdoch
> crawling over Fleet Street, a pygmy King Kong –
> did they shrug off an empire for this?

The demotic "shrug off" is characteristic of Tranter's irreverence. Indeed, Tranter is a great producer of polemic; though whether the polemic produced is great is another matter. The poems in *Urban Myths: 210 Poems* – a halfway house between a *Collected* and a *Selected* poems – are iconoclastic; make stabs at tendentiousness; are riddled with self-conscious

metapoetic references and an awareness of What-it-means-to-be-a-poet –
particularly a modern Australian poet. Porter's words thus feel incongruous
when encountered here. Despite their shared sense of nationality, these are
two very different writers. Tranter's poetry is a catalogue of absurd
paraphernalia; it is not hewn out of the Australian landscape, but out of a
plethora of things, objects and processes: "cobalt milkshake", "infra-red
photometry", "metaphysics on the phosphor screen", "photo-realist
wallpaper".

"I find myself alone in a room full of stupid poems" is an apt line from
a 1976 opus entitled 'The Alphabet Murders', a twenty-seven part sequence
of sprawling shards of free verse. This line, which opens the ninth shard,
encapsulates rather too perfectly the experience of reading this sequence: a
sense of bemusement and yes, boredom. When Tranter goes on to write:
"and like some long and boring poem by Matthew Arnold [....]" the reader
becomes aware of the desire to remove the 'T' from his surname. Tranter is
much better when he abandons free verse and adopts the sonnet form.
Modernised and for the most part unrhymed, these are terse and
epigrammatic. 'Artefact' spins words in circles and plays on its title,
pondering the meanings of the words "art" and "fact". 'Ballistics' uses a
Miltonic rhyme scheme as a framework; the rhyming on words relating to
everyday banalities undercuts the tragedy of the poem's mini-narrative with
a sly wryness.

These sonnets work for Tranter because they have a sense of resolve.
But it is the lack of resolution elsewhere in the collection that most separates
Tranter's work from Peter Porter's. *Eighteen Poems* is a low-key gem; full of
irreverence and grace. The opening poem, 'Rendering a Rochester
Fragment', is structured and substantial; formalist in its use of rhyming
couplets, but the subtlety of its rhyming gives it fluidity and prevents
anachronism or monotony. Interspersed with italicised fragments, the
poem examines theological ontology:

> The gods make speeches, dust-dry monologues,
> Loquacious oracles, extended blogs,
> All emanating in heroic mist,
> Not one an actor but ventriloquist
> Of their dependents, this humanity,
> No line his own, each praised by you and me.

Here too there is persistent self-reflexive reference to being a poet, and the
poet's craft. In 'Troupiez, Troupiez', Porter sets out a manifesto of sorts for

writing poetry:

> Would love to make this prime confession
> A new creation of my own – find sharp
> Caesuras unexpectedly; avoid
> Five feet, conveyor-belt iambics, rhyme
> Intrinsically and yet eccentrically,
> And claim a pioneering dialect
> In which the tribe might customise itself.

Everything hangs in abeyance until this last line. The aspirations expressed in this 'manifesto' may be poetic commonplaces; well-rehearsed desires for perfection and recognition. It is the conclusion, with its resonant word "tribe", that is arresting. It suggests a small community, a sense of close collusion; a sense of this Eliotian community establishing a dialect, or a voice within a poetic context. This acts as a statement of intent; an intent to find a place for Australian poetry, with its perceived youth, alongside older traditions. Porter is clearly already successful in this respect – and so he is able to ask:

> How did you get in, confront the tracery
> Beyond the boarded-up high window
> To fly so gaily past the painted sky?

There is a thesis waiting to be written about this tradition of "high windows" in modern poetry: the image appears in a Sylvia Plath poem some thirty years before Larkin uses it. Porter ends his poem with the unanswered question: "How will you find your way out now you're in?" His high window is "boarded-up", not made of "sun-comprehending glass"; it is a symbol of enclosure rather than of aperture and transcendence.

In Robert Gray's new collection, *Nameless Earth*, there is an exquisite eclogue for Sylvia Plath. As the collection's title suggests, Gray's poems often present a kind of pastoral, with a keen attention to detail:

> I find your grave
> is small, child-like;
> you've always seemed
> claustrophobic,

but this – too sad
as final ground;
such narrowness
un-American.

Although he insists that he "has no taste for / romanticism", Gray
undermines this assertion time and again. Set against Tranter's cynicism,
Gray certainly seems something of a Romantic, with his luscious compound
adjectival phrases: "red-lipped", "storm-bitten", "junket-coloured", "dew-
lapped", "breast-tipped", "sand-tipped", "fog-bound", "bat-plagued". Indeed,
after Tranter's attic-collection it is pleasant to open Gray's collection on a
poem entitled simply 'Gardenias'; a poem in which aspects of the natural
world are richly depicted, and merged with aspects of the material world:

a harsh typewriter
sound of wetness, and bougainvillea
wound as lianas, sawn away between
each carved post.

The past participle "wound" could be read as the noun "wound", meaning
"cut"; which introduces an idea of natural bloom and decay that is carried
through to the end of the poem, "into this richness of rotting flowers." Here
too, the medium for this perception of "richness" is "open windows".

Robert Gray seems to answer Peter Porter's question, "How will you
find your way out now you're in?" when he writes, in 'Voyage':

[...] We can find

no way because
outside is unstable, the same

as within us –
in all the worlds

there is no escape from sorrow.

Despite this seemingly pessimistic last line, Gray distils this sense of
precarious belonging into clipped two-line stanzas, bridging the gap
between outer and inner realities with the stanzaic enjambment.

In *The Biplane Houses*, Les Murray is more optimistic about the identity of the Australian poet. He writes, casually, "I was upstaged in Nottingham / after reading poetry there [...]". It transpires that he has been upstaged by the presence of eight "ginger human skeletons" in the room above; some of whom, he considers, might have been his ancestors, "Nottingham / being where my mother's people fled from // in the English Civil War." As an Australian looking into Britain, Murray finds a way to root himself in his new surroundings, in the fragments of his own history that he finds there. This collection is characterised by joy and joviality as he weaves myths and histories out of landscape; and populates both panoramic and domestic vistas with likely and unlikely characters.

Often incongruous groups of people from different times and places are thrown into Murray's line of vision: "Wesleyans", "Ossianic Celts", "neo-Polynesians", "GIs and Hemingways" shake hands across the poems, despite the strangeness of their juxtaposition. This pan-cultural optimism and whimsicality characterises these poems. 'The Physical Diaspora of William Wallace', despite its gruesome premise, renders the subject of dismemberment vaguely comical by laying it out in concise rhymed quatrains, making a sort of anti-blazon:

> and my heart's in the Highlands,
> my spleen is in York,
> one gnawed shin's in London,
> my blood's in your talk –

Murray has created a dark nursery rhyme: a lyric that could be chanted by children, yet one that carries with it questions of identity and cross-cultural violence, the erosion and the re-establishment of cultural identity.

'Twelve Poems' is a collection of aphorisms in tercets, almost Haiku-like, which shift in tone from one verse to the next – from earnest sincerity to the near-saccharine, from baffling to tenderly humorous – culminating in: "Filling in a form / the simple man asks his mother / *Mum, what sex are we*?" The neo-Communist 'The Cool Green' is a slew of disenchantment featuring phrases such as "we are money's genitals" and ending with the wounded idealism of "How did money capture life / away from poetry, ideology, religion?" Murray's greatest moments in this book come when he avoids polemic. His visionary strength is captured beautifully in 'The Domain of the Octopus':

> Octopus, rider of sea-level
> up and down the Ice Ages:

once she embraced river ports
in still-unfocussed country

where black and white were extremes.
That merger of skins began a nation
soon snubbed out of existing.
One day its boat will come in.

Centuries of human civilisation are condensed into two quatrains, without fighting each other for space in which to breathe and expand. It seems appropriate that Murray achieves the optimism of this last line – when he has constructed so masterful a poetic vision with which to do so.

Charlotte Newman is at Selwyn College, Cambridge.

℘

Imaginary Republics

PAUL BATCHELOR

Martín Espada, *The Republic of Poetry*,
Norton, hb. $23.95, ISBN 9780393062564;
Durs Grünbein, translated by Michael Hoffman, *Ashes for Breakfast*,
Faber, £12.99, ISBN 0571228496;
Mervyn Morris, *I been there, sort of: New & Selected Poems*,
Carcanet, £9.95, ISBN 1857548299;
Togara Muzanenhamo, *Spirit Brides*, Carcanet, £7.95, ISBN 1857548523

Durs Grünbein was born in Dresden in 1962. Today, his country of origin only exists insofar as its conditions have been internalised, and *Ashes for Breakfast* is characterised by a dream-like sense of dislocation. This inner exile permits neither relief or nostalgia, favouring instead a wry gallows humour. For example, in 'Variations on No Theme' a man shaving is described as "an animal / In double jeopardy, practicing / The use of edged tools while standing on its hindlegs".

These translations often recall the poetry of their translator, Michael Hoffman (who cites Lowell's example in his introduction), but as this is not a bilingual edition we cannot gauge the extent to which this is due to appropriation or shared concerns. What is certain is how well the translations work as poems in their own right. Deftly switching between registers, and with a typically cynical swagger, 'All About You' accumulates details of a grimy urban landscape, building to the image of a "flock of mangy pigeons" resembling:

> the bespattered extras in an
> assassination flick (*The*
> *Murder of Leo Trotsky*) or the usual
> BBBBBB films… but instead you just
> gander on very slowly
> to the next crossing, because
> today is all about you.

Brilliant as they are, the early, self-contained poems come to look like inspired sketches for the more ambitious later sequences. I'll leave you with this, from the wonderful 'Greetings from Oblivion City':

> Suicide is accounted a crime. Anyone to whom an interest
> In self-murder is imputed (say, by kindly neighbours)
> Has only moments before a lawman shoots him dead.
> You can vote for anything, it seems, but not for death.

Grünbein's cynicism would be anathema to Martín Espada, a much-lauded Brooklyn-born poet, translator and editor of an anthology of Latino poetry, who believes in poetry's socio-political duty. Unfortunately, despite Espada's admirable real-life radicalism, the poems in *The Republic of Poetry* are rhythmically flat and lacking in surprising images: in the title poem, poets "scream for joy" while the people are "blinded by grief". When Espada tries for something more adventurous, the results are often infelicitous, as when Neruda's mourners are described as having "lips sewn up by the seamstress grief". Characteristically, this image is not sustained beyond the line break. The most satisfying poem is the most atypical in this regard: in 'City of Glass' Espada finds an image that can hold his attention.

Espada claims to celebrate the power of poetry, but it would be truer to say he celebrates poets. Yusef Komunyakaa is serenaded: "we have no words for you; / there is no name for the grief in your face […]" and the sequence describing a visit to Chile makes Espada's aspirations clear:

> a man with stonecutter's hands
> lifted up his boy of five

so the boy's eyes could search mine.
Son, the father said, *this is a poet,*
like Pablo Neruda.
('Black Islands.')

But Neruda is valued because he wrote memorable poems; Espada has not done this here. It is a bitter paradox that poets flourish under persecution, while nothing silences them like reverence. Excessive regard for forebears and a wish to speak for (rather than challenge) a constituency leads to platitudes, not poetry.

In 'A Poet of the People' Mervyn Morris registers his disdain for poets who foreground "loud and clear" meaning in return for "immediate applause". Instead, Morris opts for "smouldering restraint". He shows what this can achieve in 'Post-colonial Identity':

The language they're conducted in
dictates the play of these debates.
Good English, as they say, discriminates.
White people language white as sin.

Here, each word has been weighed judiciously: that "as they say" is priceless. It is only fair to say that not every poem in *I been there, sort of: New and Selected Poems* is so rewarding. Many are short missives like 'Eve':

the garden
seemed

a proper
paradise

until
she buck up

on a serpent
talking nice

This seems too content with its own transience, with only the Jamaican locution "buck up" to hold our attention, though even here Morris's worldview is likeable enough to draw the reader on, and his poems gather a cumulative power.

Morris smoulders most brightly in the poems which open the second half of this book. 'The Pond' and 'Shadowboxing' contain more openly angry work, and 'On Holy Week' is an ambitious sequence, spoken by various characters from the story of the Crucifixion. These re-visionary monologues return Judas, Doubting Thomas, Pilate *et al* to an identifiable human context. The concept that poems might be vehicles for ideas seems currently out of fashion in Britain; allowing for it is one of many valuable adjustments we should expect to make when reading a fine English language poet from an international tradition.

Togara Muzanenhamo's *Spirit Brides* is an impressively assured debut. His poems favour fractured narratives (as distinct from anecdotes) and are written in long lines that cross and re-cross the borders of prose-poetry, utilizing speech-rhythms without becoming prosaic. Muzanenhamo grew up in Zimbabwe and is well-travelled, so his subject matter is broad. A natural story-teller, he has the confidence not to signpost a poem's significance. For example, 'Strangers' describes queuing for days for petrol in Zimbabwe. The poem takes its time, apparently idling like the queue, but alert to minute changes in the men's watchful camaraderie:

> Someone mentions a journey to South Africa –
> Then talk of the cricket,
> The World Cup and how the boys are faring,
> Then the news.
> An awkward silence.
> No one says what they're thinking,
> Realising we're amongst strangers.

The collection's finest achievement is 'Gumiguru', a long prose poem concerning Muzanenhamo's father's funeral, but excerpts would not do it justice. Here instead is the final stanza of 'The Last Days of Winter', displaying characteristically exact observation and a fully inhabited language:

> […] frost scars the windowpanes framing the milk-spilt sea, the glass
> Splintered and cracked by the wind's horned rage. Now, no more
> > > words
> Rise to the ceiling in the dark, just warm movements of love where
> A polished sigh shoots up like a spark and bursts into the wrestle of
> > > a fuck.

Paul Batchelor's *To Photograph a Snow Crystal* was published by Smith Doorstop in 2006.

Guilty Of Dust And Sin

MELANIE CHALLENGER

Anne Carson, *Decreation*, Cape, £12, ISBN 9780224079263;
Maxine Kumin, *Jack and Other New Poems*,
Norton, £8.99, ISBN 9780393328523

Anne Carson's first collection in five years inherits its title from the mystical philosophy of Simone Weil. Though the back cover tells us that this 'Decreation' begins in the "undoing of form," there is more profound undoing of self by the author, an ecstatic undoing with sexual overtones: "*ekstasis*, literally 'standing outside oneself,' a condition regarded by the Greeks as typical of mad persons, geniuses and lovers, and ascribed to poets by Aristotle."

The collection opens on 'Sleepchains', a short poem whose "cicatrice" turns out to be a diacritical mark of struggle. Poems lead into an essay, in "praise of sleep", which retells the return of Odysseus to Penelope: "Homer has woven a strange symbiosis between these two people, together and apart in the same night, entering and exiting each other's minds, almost sharing one consciousness – especially at the moment when Penelope penetrates the membrane of her husband's sleep and fills him with joy. I would call that a successful seduction." This scene finds its counterpart in an essay on fourteenth-century Frenchwoman Marguerite Porete, burned at the stake for writing a heretical book about her love of God: "At the moment of annihilation [...] God practices upon the soul an amazing act of ravishing. For God opens an aperture in the soul and allows divine peace to flow in upon her like glorious food." Now I would call *that* a successful seduction.

Carson ends this section with an 'Ode to Sleep' which turns into an ode on the struggle for meaning, wrested from a kind of god, if not God. The last line summons the character of Jacob, from the Abrahamic religions, whose nightlong struggle with a divine being leaves its mark upon his thigh: "It hurts me to know this / Exit wound, as they say." The allusion is underpinned by the notes that accompany the section. Carson's sources include Aristotle's *On Prophecy in Sleep* – which reads sleep and dreams "as messages from the realm of the daimonic, which lies between divine and human bring" – as well as the scene between Odysseus and Penelope referred to earlier, where "Odysseus is recognized by his old nurse Eurykleia because of the scar on his leg."

As if carried by the uncanny interconnectivity of Carson's own dream-world, we progress to a section on the Sublime, landscaped by Fuseli's *Nightmare*, in which "to feel the joy of the sublime is to be inside creative power for a moment, to share a bit of electric extra life with the artist's invention, to spill with him." (Less dark horse than 'dark swallow' here, the seed of the ravishing creator.) Through a myriad bizarre and frequently witty forms and subjects, from opera libretti to film transcripts, Longinus to Antonioni, Carson makes "a little rip in our minds" through which, if we surrender ourselves, enters the joy of meanings suggested by these links of logic, these dream-emblems.

The philosophy of Simone Weil teaches us that "The only way into truth is through one's own annihilation," and this annihilation is an absurd act, an imitation of God's absence from the universe of his making, which she termed a 'Decreation': "As a child, for a joke, hides behind an armchair from his mother, God plays at separating himself from God through creation. We are this joke of God's." Thus God struggles with himself and yields the cicatrice that is man; for Carson, this cicatrice is her own volumes. Struggling against the American confessional tradition that precedes her, Carson seeks solace in this 'Decreation', remarking, "My personal poetry is a failure. / I do not want to be a person." To which the reader can only respond that this then must be her impersonal work, since it is assuredly not a failure. The 'exit wound' is sealed.

In *Jack and Other New Poems* Maxine Kumin – though not the strong poet that is Anne Carson – engages in her own act of 'decreation', in a series of poems that witness the undoing of life in death, the natural world in decay, the poetic output in oblivion. These are modest, laudatory poems, whose virtue lies in the tension created by the way her lusty, life-affirming language is pressed into service to the rites of death, a struggle of which she has "yet to let go." A deft ending links Kumin's collection to Anne Carson's, for the final question of her *Sonnet in So Many Words*, "Can you taste it?", summons the poem 'Love' by George Herbert. 'Love' happened to be the favourite poem of French philosopher, Simone Weil; who knew these final lines, "You must sit downe, sayes Love, and taste my meat / So I did sit and eat," by heart.

Melanie Challenger's first collection is *Galatea* (Salt, 2006). She won an Eric Gregory Award in 2005.

℘

Small Press Round-Up

Tim Turnbull, *Stranded in Sub-Atomica*, Donut Press,
£10, ISBN 0954198360; Roz Goddard, *How to Dismantle a Hotel Room*,
Coalpress Publishing, £7, ISBN 0955376602; Chris Emery, *Radio Nostalgia*,
Arc Publications, £8.99, ISBN 1904604191; Kathryn Maris, *The Book of Jobs*,
Four Way Books, $14.95, ISBN 1884800718; Andrew Duncan, *Savage
Survivals amid modern suavity*, Shearsman Books, £8.95,
ISBN 1905700032; Andy Brown, *Fall of the Rebel Angels*, Salt, £9.99, ISBN
184471280X; Richard Burns, *The Blue Butterfly*, Salt, £10.99, ISBN
1844712583; Fred Beake, *New and Selected Poems*, Shearsman, £8.95, ISBN
0907652981; Frank Ormsby (ed.) *The Blackbird's Nest*, Blackstaff, £9.99,
ISBN 0856407968; Jibanananda Das, *Bengal the Beautiful* (tr. Joe Winter),
Anvil, £8.95, ISBN 0856463906; Ernst Jandl, *Dingfest/Thingsure*, (tr. Michael
Hamburger), Dedalus, £7.50, ISBN 1904556566; Liu Hongbin, *A Day Within
Days*, Ambit Books, £6.95, ISBN 0900055103; Mario Petrucci, *Catullus*,
Perdika Press, £4.50 ISBN 1905649002; Peter Robinson, *Talk About Poetry:
Conversations on the Art*, Shearsman, ISBN 1905700042, £9.95.

Tim Turnbull's *Stranded in Sub-Atomica* is a high-octane collection
that reverberates with acerbic wit and a sense that this poet takes no
prisoners. 'Chainsaw' typifies his approach. It takes Simon Armitage's
'Chainsaw versus the Pampas Grass' and uses it to make a technically astute
– and cutting – poem which demonstrates not only Turnbull's intimacy with
chainsaws but also his control of the forces he is capable of bringing to bear
on verse. There is satire certainly; Armitage's 'chainsaw' is reduced to a toy by
comparison; but there is also the linguistic force of the poem which could so
easily have been overdone if attempted by a poet without Turnbull's talent.
He can control the snarling beast he unleashes – just:

> And he won't have fought the gyroscopic thrust
> of the engine and the juddering Oregon chain
> or snatched his lever, shouldered up and pushed [...]

But Turnbull is not just about satire and slick vernacular; he is capable of
subtle formal technique. His rhymes in 'Sea Monster' and 'Archie Rice with
Everything' are muted, understated. He demonstrates expert formal control

in 'Not the Whitsun Weddings.' He uses the sonnet inventively in 'The Touring Shakespeare Company's Visit is Eagerly Awaited in Grozny in 1953' and couplets with consummate ease in 'The Men from U.N.C.O.O.L.' Tim Turnbull is a truly cutting-edge poetic talent. To borrow an analogy, Turnbull has a chainsaw and he knows it's a chainsaw...

Roz Goddard's *How to Dismantle a Hotel Room* contains some highly achieved work. This is a voice capable of modulation. Goddard uses pathos and humour as well as sophisticated control within versification to achieve a quiet yet profound effect. Most of these poems are very well wrought indeed. In 'A Meal at Peter's', Goddard vividly delivers a sense of awkwardness, class division and social embarrassment: "I'd carry on chewing, even when there was nothing / in my mouth, nothing but air." She tempers this with humour, however, using it to convey undisguised jealousy: "Even the seven year old had something witty to say. / Brat." One feels clearly the discomfort of social ineptitude. Goddard is very good at such up-close and personal narration. 'A Falling', too, works because it is a personal love poem from the poet to her city. The images are specific, tight and loaded with personal significance:

> 'Bend close' you say and you will see the specks
> of brilliance walked into pavements,
> left as routinely as the memory of snow.

Chris Emery's language is dense and has been pared down to convey the stark nature of the world and the taut lives of the characters which people his particular wasteland. As a collection, *Radio Nostalgia* thrives on the binding device of this tight diction. In places it is so contracted as to do away with articles and prepositions; creating an interesting linguistic effect that springs the rhythm of the entire language and renders it foreign – as in 'Henry Purcell's Love Song':

> And barking purple cells
> show gold night gold
> day and tell us [...]

Not all the poems are quite as densely-packed as this, but the collection does have a rather breathless feel to it generally, through the preponderance of very short lines, which presumably Emery feels convey the urgency and sense of impending panic which pervade the book.

This is not to say that he doesn't vary the fare. He uses the longer line very effectively in poems like 'Clan Tinnitus' and 'From the Centre'. The latter, particularly, allows a much more musical and expansive, breathier feel to the verse – with its pervasive assonances and internal rhymes. Likewise, in Kathryn Maris's *The Book of Jobs*, I found much that worked well. Poems like 'Door' and 'Opthalmology at Dawn' successfully question language and perception while also allowing the reader direct access to the imagery and narrative:

> The retina is a forest at dusk
> reddening beneath the beaming
> optic disc.

In the best poems there is also an edginess and a feeling of movement outside the comfort zone: "an unmissed boy at midnight. His understated knife".

Savage Survivals is an apt title for much of the post-modern linguistic experimentation going on in Andrew Duncan's new collection. I like the way Duncan goes about his work. It is not grimly serious and 'up itself'. His images are clean and bold; he trusts them to communicate with the reader without the need for overt filtering authorial presence. Even where there is a strong 'I', it is an observing 'eye' rather than a directing 'I':

> I could feel my mind seeping out through my skin
> To fill the room as a rare grey cube
> An hour of bloody excess. Moonlight on a dulled blade.

There is humour and rhythm and a sense of play. That lightness of touch makes it much easier to bear some of the grimmer work because it is offset by work which makes one smile or laugh out loud, as I did at 'Bob Cob Bing Bong':

> gob in a bungle and at'em snore
> a cement-mixer being raped by a warthog
> a concrete masher being mixed by a wart-peeler
> a book being wrapped by a Concrete Quaker.

Andy Brown's selection from his last ten years of work, *Fall of the Rebel Angels*, is a smorgasbord of tensile images. Brown has linguistic originality and delights in experiments with form. My particular favourites from this very achieved collection were the prose poems; which showed best of all his love of language and his willingness to play with music, meaning and the reader's expectations and perceptions. Elsewhere, Richard Burns's *The Blue*

Butterfly is a magnificent book. It uses seven tightly-worked subsections to examine a massacre at Šumarice in 1941. The volume is suffused with hope and bravery; and examines ethnic cleansing and mass hatred in a way that is particularly relevant in the current political climate. Fred Beake's *New and Selected Poems* gathers together the best of over thirty-five years of work into a volume which exhibits the variety of styles and voices to which this versatile poet can adapt. In *The Blackbird's Nest*, Frank Ormsby gathers together over fifty poets who have been associated with Queens University over the last century. This is a celebration of poetry itself and demonstrates the quality of poets that Queen's has attracted or produced over the last hundred years or so.

Also received were several volumes of versions and translations: Joe Winter's translations of the Bengali poet Jinanananda Das, *Bengal The Beautiful*; a re-issue from Dedalus Press of Michael Hamburger's tightly wrought translations of Ernst Jandl, *Dingfest/Thingsure*; Liu Hongbin's translations of his own work in co-operation with Peter Porter and others, *A Day within Days;* and versions of Catullus rendered into modern idiom by Mario Petrucci. I would also like to draw attention to Peter Robinson's enlightening collection of interviews gathered together over about a decade, *Talk about Poetry: Conversations on the Art.*

Nigel McLoughlin's 'Night Fire' appears on p. 48.

The Corneliu M Popescu Prize For Poetry Translation 2007

Sponsored by the Ratiu Family Charitable Foundation

This prize is open to collections of poetry published between April 2005 and May 2007 which feature poetry translated from another European language into English.

The judges for this year are Anne Born and Francis Jones. The prize is £1000.

The deadline for submissions is 31 May, 2007. To submit book(s) send three copies of the publication to Popescu Prize, 22 Betterton Street, London, WC2H 9BX.

The prize is named after Corneliu M Popescu, a young Romanian translator killed in an earthquake in 1977.

To find out more telephone 020 7420 9880 or email competition@poetrysociety.org.uk Visit www.poetrysociety.org.uk

---

THE GEOFFREY DEARMER PRIZE 2006

Tamara Fulcher has won this year's Geoffrey Dearmer Prize: awarded to an emerging poet, who has not yet published a full collection, for work appearing in *Poetry Review*. This year's prize was judged by the poet, librettist and fiction writer David Harsent.

Tamara Fulcher, who is twenty-nine, grew up in Kent but has lived in Scotland since taking her degree, an MA (Hons) in Ancient History at Edinburgh University. Her poetry has been appearing in magazines since 2004. She is working on a novel, *The Past and Sorrow of Lenny J*, which – with the poem-cycle *Yellow* – is her key project for 2007. Her first collection, *The Recreation of Night*, will be published by Shearsman Books in 2008. David Harsent praised Tamara Fulcher's winning poem, 'Choirsinger', saying: "This bleak little domestic drama of loss and loneliness is cleverly understated. In fact, its tragedy lies in restraint: an economy that extends into technique. [...] The narrator breaks off, now and then, to punctuate the poem with intense images that characterise the event and act as counterpoint to a series of utterances the sheer banality of which is, ironically, an indicator of their power to hurt. You can almost hear the echoes. [...] The level tone of the piece gives everything away: the fear of feeling, the expectation of neglect; and the lines find just the right weight to allow us to witness the little tableau, static for only a moment, the arrested motion, the averted eyes, the damage done, the damage yet to come."

The Geoffrey Dearmer Prize is awarded, through the generosity of the Dearmer family, to honour the noted World War One poet and Society member. *Poetry Review* is extremely grateful to the Dearmer family and to David Harsent. Fulcher's winning poem appeared in *PR 95:4: The Music of It*.

Tamara Fulcher
Titanic (explained by *Mer*)

I shoved up one finger
and tore a hole along her side
black, but the red showed underneath

and she inbled, letting my laugh
run into her and weigh her

                down
                down
                upended upturn and crack

                an iron shell remains a shell

I was taking back
my pearls

Two Ugly Carpet Fitters

It's been over a year now,
so don't be surprised,

and besides, I've always been fascinated
by men with unusual gaits, and you walked
as though unaware someone had nicked
your spacehopper. And you were blond, and curly,

unusual for me, but there you go. Refer
to the above. Anyway, I gave you the bigger
one, since you were clearly the apprentice,
stuck with fixing gripper around my toilet

and not allowed to handle cash. So I pulled
you in by it, and your boss is married,
I know because he told me. Actually he didn't,
but he did say, "We've got a 2 year-old, too,"

and I don't expect he meant him and you.
Regardless. Boss: you followed, kind of licking
your mouth and turning gay, a little,
opportunistically of course, and I became

suddenly ambidextrous with your
tracksuit ties and shirtholes, and pretty soon
I was roasting. Less a desperate housewife
than a hard-legged bronze, feeling altruistic

and I have Buttermilk on my bathroom floor
and number 80753/9 in the kitchen,
I have it all ways and more, I tip 20%
even though your hammering knocks chips

out of my white skirting, even though you
hammered the screws into the doorbar, while
I watched, and I'll tell you I was thinking,
"Is that what they call a Glasgow screwdriver?"

but never said it. Too busy not making eyes
at married Boss and listening to you
singing to each other upstairs, and going
red, and not liking the vinyl after all,

so that when you'd waved from the door,
Blond, kind of sarcastic because I didn't tip
at all, not even enough for a pint on the
drive home, so that when you'd bounced

(always bouncing) away down the hall
I got my hammer and I got my knife and I
cut it all out, cut the hide from the skin
and black-bagged it up, this went on just

most of the night and here I am,
two months later, nobody's been in
since you, and Boss, you weren't so awful,
a bit on the short side but I know what

I've heard about that, and Blond was surely
ugly but you all look the same with my
eyes closed, so I left the chips to make me
think of you, in the afternoons.

It's been more than a year now,
riding my hand.

NATIONAL POETRY COMPETITION 2006

First Prize
Mike Barlow
The Third Wife

My first wife knew no more than me, no telling
where her needs ended, mine began. One day though
I turned the hill to find the boat moored in the field,
the house out in the bay, adrift, door open wide.
I rowed out to a message on the mat: gone
to my cousin's place in Valparaiso.

My second wife blew ashore in a force ten
leading a shipload of apprentices astray
with her white dress, her turned-up Nordic nose,
her precious bible clutched in a manicured hand.
No matter how I pumped, the organ of her heart played flat,
her painted smile as wooden as a figurehead's.

My third wife won't say where she lives.
She comes to me when the tides are right,
stays longer if a wind's got up or fog's come down.
I stroke the warm loaves of her biceps, kiss
dimpled elbows, listen for the souch
our breathing makes when we're together.

She has cousins everywhere. They post her money
in denominations the local shop won't take
or drop by uninvited while we're having tea. They push me
into corners, whisper her address. I turn a deaf ear.
This is my third wife I explain, who's known
many husbands, some worse some better than me.

Second Prize

John Latham
From Professor Hobu Kitagawa's Notebooks
On Effects Of Lightning On The Human Body

Tr. from the Japanese by N. Kitagawa

89. Incident on the Horikiko Coast (30/07/78)
Young couple alone, he recumbent on red rock
near pinnacle of sand-hill pocketed with grass,
she by his feet, sky making threat of raindrops
though earth remaindered dry. Mid-afternoon,
adjacent to sun's zenith, she touching ground
at plural potions of her body, while lightning
conflaged cracked dead-bush 6m from stone,
surge entering body by left toe and knee-skins
scorched but hardly. Consciousness abandoned
but resumed itself to her beyond thirty minutes
bequeathing no damage but burn marks, livid
at spine terminus, shaping like shouting throat.
Her memories of suction into light fibrillating
like new leaves. Man felt no perverse effects,
seven heart-flowers uncorrupted in his hand,
though since he suffers rapture of tympanum.

213. Higashi-Yuri-Machi Incident (22/09/97)
In Takaiwa-Yama, summer's declining parts,
school-teacher of language and nine-year son
relaxing in garden by lotus pool at light-fade,
playing go. No hailstones, no St. Elmo's Fire,
so foreboding invalid, yet flash strick jay-tree
20m distance, beneath whose roots iron pipe
reclined, convoying pool-water at arid times.
Predominant currents swept below go-board
and players either side, with subsidiary flow
up left leg of father, departing from his body

at index, central fingers of right hand almost
touching board. They badly cindered, fused,
yet still holding black stone for further play.
There is death in the ha-ne, as proverb says.
Boy hurtled into water, naked as carried out,
unscathed except for fern prints on left heel.

Third Prize
David Grubb
Bud Fields And His World

i.m. James Agee

What are you going to tell us, Bud;
about the days that keep coming and
rain and wind and the sour smell of shacks
and empty fields and the silence of women?

How do you look your children in the eye
and what stories can there possibly be to
hide the intimidation, the neglect that nails
you and the stench of what you wear inside?

Let us now praise insects that survive and winter
grass and the ways the bed travels and the boy
with the broken head who keeps singing and how
the moon seems to care in occasional dreams.

Let us praise the locust and some birds and those
who know how a book works and the man who
sits in a field with some children and says it is
a special place where the light can become song.

What is song, Bud; what is its persistence when some
yell it from a distance and some hide inside a hymn
and even your own children listen to its sway and
how it rocks the soul if you let it in?

What is it, Bud; keeping you here between days and
the nights that that are useless and the junk that you
hear some other men speaking and the solace that
every so often appears when your wife lets you in?

Let us praise the far distance and the biggest star
and the river that lives forever and the way a child
makes a game with some rope and the way that you
can some days see your mother inspecting her hands.

In the photograph you stare straight ahead, Bud;
what do you think this is all about? Are they going to
pay you? Are they going to ask you to say? Anything.
Anything they might possible understand. What words

are you going to use, to tell, to share, to cut out an image
that they can take to others? Talk of what and to make
what happen when nothing will? Wind. Rain. Dead dogs.
Tell us about dead dogs and how you keep hearing them.

Tell us about earth and the hot nights and the no sleeping
and the scream of the father who returns to swear at you
and the way you cannot even remember him whistling and
how he never even praised a thing. Never ever did praise.

ॐ

Poetry Review is glad to follow the annual tradition of publishing the three
winning poems from the Poetry Society's National Poetry Competition. In
this, its twenty-ninth year, the judges were John Burnside, Lee Harwood and
Alice Oswald. The competition attracts up to 10,000 entries annually; and
this year in addition to the winners there were ten commendations. John
Burnside says: "Judging a single-poem competition can be frustrating in the
current climate. One finds a good poem and wants to read more of that
writer's work, one longs for the complete collection, for the back catalogue.
Yet it is oddly appropriate that our national poetry competition should
revolve around a single moment, a single idea or vision because this, surely,
is what we prize most in the lyric: that momentary attention to detail, that
quiet glimmer of understanding, that sense of a particular here-and-now
captured in a single, beautifully discovered metaphor."

ENDPAPERS

Julia Casterton 1952-2007

It is with great regret that we learn, as we go to press, of the death of Julia Casterton. One of our most committed teachers of creative writing – as her publications demonstrate – Casterton won the Jerwood Aldeburgh First Collection Prize in 2004 for *The Doves of Finisterre*. She was recently awarded an Arts Council of England Bursary, and in recent poems, such as 'Goblins' which appeared in the last issue of *PR*, gave readers an insight into her own illness.

Goblins

It can take eons to get rid of them.
You lie half-conscious in a hospital bed.
Strong hands fill you up with glucose, blood and iron.
Yet the memory of goblins sucking out your womb,

your bone marrow,
won't leave you. By day you doze,
at night you fight them in your body,
a *lucha continua*.

Your vision fades, sense fails, you float
on the chance their antics in last night's parade
signal that they are bored, and might move on
to another foolish eater, suicide, or sister.

EDITORIAL

FIONA SAMPSON

In her *Letter from Beirut*, Joumana Haddad suggests that the Arab world (pop. 270 million) boasts 20,000 poets and 9,720 readers. It's a paradox familiar wherever participation in poetry means *composing* it. In the West, too, the Romantic legacy seems to imply that poetry arises from and addresses a wellspring of irreplaceably personal experience. Of course, while the Romantics went on to claim poets were characterised by exceptional intensity, modernity acknowledges the democracy of emotion. Patience Strong was right! We're all seized by griefs and joys. And poetry's *apartness* – whether from gossip or scholarship or therapy – allows it to resonate with these heightened experiences.

What sets poetry apart, whether musically or semantically, seems to have something to do with beauty, and with risk. Beauty in verse is in any case always risky. It entails self-disclosure: a poet reveals what they find beautiful. This is *not* cool. And it runs the risk of misjudgement; all writing which extends itself runs the risk of sailing close to winds of pretension, brilliance or shock. Not *correct*. Yet work which doesn't run such risk is – the term's advised – *prosaic*. There's an element of real struggle and discomfort in the business of composition.

If it's so hard, why do it? Well, here's a risky proposition: perhaps *poetry's written to be read*. Where I live, there are always kids kicking a ball about. They all dream of being the next Wayne Rooney. They never miss The Match. The continuum between what they do and what their team does on-screen is urgently alive. And football is the global sport. So, as poetry enters the orbit of inevitable 2012 Olympic overspend, what might we learn from them?

At the time of writing, the axe already hangs over *London Magazine* (founded 1732): that home of new writing which early championed Sylvia Plath, Harold Pinter and Derek Walcott. The annual £30,000-odd saved, should it remain in literature, could doubtless fund a couple of community residencies; each enabling a total of (let's say) eighty people to participate in (for example) four weekly workshops. But my hunch is that *LM* has rather more than a hundred-and-sixty readers. And – yes – reading *is* participation. Any serious poet will tell you reading is essential to them. More importantly, so will any *lover* of poetry. It's on behalf of such poetry-lovers that *Poetry Review*, with its mission to publish the best writing in Britain today, continues to work.

Letter from Beirut

JOUMANA HADDAD

Poetry is proof that life is not enough
– Fernando Pessoa

To be is not easy. Hamlet said so it in the 1600s. And here we are, still learning how to do it in 2007. More and more expensively, may I add.

To be a poet is quite complicated, to say the least. We belong to an endangered species which is not best equipped for a risk-free life on planet Earth. And don't think I'm indulging myself in the *"You cannot write poetry unless you have a miserable life"* cliché. Quite the contrary. I'm a frustrated Epicurean poet who wants to be happy. I just don't know how. (By the way, do you? R.S.V.P!)

Having said that, to be an Arab poet is an almost "impossible" identity to hold on to. Why? Simply because, on top of the above-mentioned, we are plagued by a catastrophic reading indicator. I'll let the numbers speak for themselves. According to recent statistics, I live in a region where less than 0.1% of its 270 million people read; where merely 40% of that depressing 0.1% read books; and where 9% of the 40% of the initial 0.1% actually read poetry...

You do the maths. That would leave us, according to my modest yet reliable calculating skills, with 9,720 people reading poetry, in an immense Arab world that *proudly* claims to have more than twenty thousand poets! Wouldn't you call that an irony? Well, you won't see any of us Arab poets laughing.

So where does that put us? It precisely "corners" us into a circle, a tiny stifling circle, where poets are a poet's only readership – that is, if he's lucky enough to have one! Add to that the difficulty of finding a local publisher, spice it up with the hopelessness of ever being translated into another language, dip it in the condescension of people towards writers in general, and towards poets in particular, and you'll have yourself a perfect five star poetic hell!

This year, Lebanon is celebrating the fiftieth anniversary of the first publication of *Shi'r* (i.e. *Poetry*), the magazine which, from the heart of pioneering Beirut, broke new ground and played a vital role in the establishment of modernity in Arab poetry, in the 'fifties of the twentieth century. This at a time when the destiny of our country is at stake, between the crows of the culture of death, and the knights of the culture of life. This at a time when destruction and violence are the prevailing rule, from Baghdad to Gaza, and beyond. This at a time when there is talk everywhere that "poetry is dying".

❧

I read back what I have written up to this line and I realize that it all seems gloomy, bitter and harsh. Yet true. So sadly true.

"Every Arab reads a quarter of a page annually" – "Only one in fifty-three books sold worldwide is a poetry collection" – "It's mostly older people who read poetry": these and other fatal facts echo ruthlessly in my head. But what are numbers for, anyway? We don't write poetry to be hip. We don't write poetry to be recognized. And we certainly don't write poetry to be famous. We write poetry to "be".

And that for me will always be the only, the crucial and the scariest question of all.

Joumana Haddad is a poet, translator and journalist and chief editor of the cultural pages in *An Nahar* newspaper. She has published five collections including *The Return of Lilith*; speaks seven languages and has published several works of translation. www.joumanahaddad.com.

CONTRIBUTORS

Moniza Alvi's most recent collection is *How The Stone found Its Voice* (Bloodaxe 2005).

Ciaran Carson's translation of the Old Irish epic, *The Táin* (Penguin Classics), appears this autumn.

John F. Deane is founder of *Poetry Ireland* and Dedalus Press. His latest collection is *The Instruments of Art* (Carcanet 2005).

Greg Delanty's latest book is *Collected Poems 1986-2006* (Carcanet).

Ruth Fainlight's most recent collection is *Moon Wheels* (Bloodaxe 2006). Her translation of Sophocles' *Theban Plays*, done with Robert Littman, is due from Johns Hopkins University Press later this year.